Yvonne

Burnt C

© Joanna Murphy 2018

Front cover concept - © The Heretic's Press
Front cover design by Chris Derrick, www.unauthorizedmedia.com

Published by The Heretic's Press
London
info@hereticspress.co.uk

Burnt Dress

© 2018 by Joanna Murphy

Published by The Heretic's Press
London

info@hereticspress.co.uk

London

By the same author

Paper Compass (poetry)
Watchman (screenplay)
The Great Duet
('The power of facial expression
& gesture in communication skills')

Joanna Murphy has asserted her moral right to be identified as the
author of this work in accordance with sections 77 and 78 of the
Copyright, Designs and Patents Act 1988.

ISBN 978-0-9567920-8-2
Kindle ISBN 978-0-9567920-9-9
2018
The Heretic's Press
www.hereticspress.co.uk

FOR J.R.M.M.

My compass

London and the countryside have been the alternating backdrops for much of Joanna Murphy's life and career, both as theatre director and writer. Born in 1958, a stone's throw from Lord's cricket ground and Regent's Park London zoo, she recalls childhood memories of hearing the lions roar in their compounds through the night. Her parents' divorce when she was very young meant a division of time between the metropolis and her father's cottage in the Welsh valleys and her mother's bases in Somerset and Hampshire.

After getting a degree in education and drama at the Froebel Institute, London Univ., she taught in the capital for a couple of years, before decamping from the UK in her twenties and going to live in Italy, where she stayed for five years. Returning to live in Oxford in the '90s, she had a son, Jack, before moving south again and enjoyed a decade-long tenure as Head of Drama at the renowned arts school, Bedales in Hampshire (where she was also Artistic Director of the Bedales Olivier Theatre). 'Burnt Dress' is her second book. She has also written a screenplay, 'Watchman', and latterly, related to her experience working with doctors in the NHS, a communication skills book, 'The Great Duet', dealing with the power of gesture, voice and facial expression in doctor-patient interactions. She is married and currently lives by the South Downs in West Sussex.

Burnt Dress

Joanna Murphy

Burnt Dress

The Heretic's Press

BURNT DRESS - CONTENTS

Part One – Motherhood and Committal

Pg.

BURNT DRESS - CONTENTS

Part Two – Growing Up in the Asylum

Pg.

Introduction

"To destroy a man's faith in himself,
that surely is the work of the Devil"
William Blake

Looked at in a certain mordant existential light, taking on the role of motherhood, with all its attendant power and frailty, constitutes an act of bravado to an almost divine degree. To hold in your arms a new human being, take it to your breast (metaphorically and/or actually) and to pronounce implicitly that this utterly dependent creature, to whom you have given life, will subsequently live or die by your hand, by the quality of your love - or lack of it!

Similarly – at the risk of courting existential absurdity - to be born of, and with, a mother could be said to tempt providence to a similarly dangerous degree! What sort of creature would submit itself to this degree of dependence? This vulnerable fate? Who are we that are born to mothers? The 'Apparitional birth' of various mythological personae is nice work if you can get it, but generally speaking those of us without divine symbolic origins will enter this world via the bodily agonies of a woman. And who knows in advance what kind of woman? Who will you get in this accident of birth? Who will she be, this fated soul you call mother, this prisoner of circumstance you condemn to the lifelong role of 'mother?'

Mine, smitten as she was (I use the word advisedly) by artistic talent and mental illness, was a spirit possessed by intensely alternating moods of light and dark. As such, I wandered every day through childhood into early adulthood in brilliant sunlight and terrifying shadow. Reflecting this, Burnt Dress is almost inevitably an ambiguous document: by turns celebratory and condemnatory, sometimes merciless, often, I hope, forgiving. Above all, I have tried to express what it is like to live with a figure so central to your life that simultaneously seems to want to nurture and destroy you.

I

Let me say immediately that I am, by and large, profoundly grateful for my lot in life. I have not been cursed by grave misfortune, have not suffered grievous physical affliction: Burnt Dress is, therefore, very definitely not a thinly-veiled cry for pity; not a belated, third-rate, so-called 'misery memoir.' I would not add my own experiences to an already over-crowded genre, one which, moreover, already boasts many literary masterpieces. Furthermore I have no doubt that I have, in the scheme of things, experienced no more misery (or ecstasy!) than the next man or woman, so to speak. But what my life very definitely has afforded me is a direct insight into a specifically dysfunctional mother/daughter relationship that usually makes or breaks the individual child involved.

For mothers and daughters present a unique challenge to each other. Potentially richly rewarding, if rarely straightforward, the relationship can be labyrinthine - a complex maze constructed from the hopes, expectations and disillusionments assembled by both parties over time. In the daughter's eyes, the mother bears the brunt of the authority figure, the mature woman and matriarch alternately admired and contemned and sometimes - such is the ambivalence of human nature - both at once - but certainly never ignored! For her part, the daughter bears the heavy burden of her mother's aspirations for her. This is, of course, natural and unavoidable. All parents inevitably have ambitions for their children, many of which are determined by the social mores of the age in which they live.

In this context, and with specific regard to the post-war decades of my youth, my mother was still largely driven by a standard set of what might loosely be called residual Victorian – even Georgian - gender values, a shamelessly pre-feminist etiquette which declared that daughters must be highly presentable, conversationally pleasant and above all marriageable. It's worth noting here that my mother had herself been unfortunate enough to be made to attend one of the last official (as it transpired), annual Queen Charlotte's Balls in the late 1950s. A woman of creative, artistic talents herself - she attended the Slade College of Art – my mother despised the mores inherent in the event, and yet could never finally shake off a vestige of credulity in them. So it was that they formed an unconscious part of the values she attempted to pass on to me.

II

As her daughter - and though obviously not formally 'inducted into society' in the way that she had been by her parents – this unconscious set of impersonal societal criteria ironically led to an intrusive, intimate scrutiny, predictably intensified when I, myself, so manifestly failed to conform to their checklist. As fate would have it, my mother's angry reactions to my (perceived) wilful nonconformity were compounded by her own Bipolar Affective Disorder (BPAD), or Manic Depression (as it was perhaps more vividly known just a generation ago): a destructive mental illness for both the sufferer and his or her dependents. Why this should be so becomes clearer on a (very) basic analysis of the condition.

By definition, bipolar sufferers access tremendous, sometimes violent extremes of mood and emotion which they are unable to control or channel in any creative, constructive way for more than the briefest period of time. Moreover, at the constant mercy of such mood swings, they rarely experience sufficient mental clarity to enable them to trace their origins back to a pathological syndrome within their own minds. On the contrary - as Jung so vividly revealed in his theory of projection - remaining unconscious of their origins, the bipolar sufferer nearly always 'projects' the causes of their moods onto other circumstances and people. In this context if a parent suffers from BPAD, then it is an unavoidable fact that family life will become the arena in which the combat of those moods is staged. Difficult enough for adults to resist, this recurrent onslaught can have disastrous results when vulnerable young children are involved.

Abandoned in the bipolar arena, the child is effectively defenceless against the daily psychological abuse perpetrated on it by the parent. Indeed, we need only substitute the word 'child' for 'man' into William Blake's above quote to begin to see how terrible the effects of a mentally ill parent on a child can be. Constantly lacerated by criticism and condemnation, over time the wounds it suffers deepen until the child begins to experience serious emotional debility – indeed, disability is not too strong a word, since its very sense of self can be crippled.

III

Of course, the above statement assumes that a bold and vigorous sense of self is a good thing to possess. I do not think this is mistaken. It seems an axiom of human nature that a belief in one's own individual worth underpins the core of one's existence. Indeed, it may also be said to be the ultimate driver of all one's endeavours in one way or another.

In one sense BPAD is a strange mental illness: deemed serious enough to require periods of compulsory hospitalisation and a lifelong dependency on various drugs to control the condition, at other times society seems happy to leave the sufferer in charge, not just of him/herself but of any dependents under their aegis.

In this context *Burnt Dress* is the narrative of what happens when the patient is left in charge of the asylum, the latter being, in this case, the family home. An admittedly extreme analogy, but I do continue to wonder why it is viewed as perfectly acceptable that children are brought up by the mentally ill in their own homes, without any outside supervision or, when necessary, intervention (indeed, one of the pieces in this book focuses on this subject).

The question may understandably be asked - where was my father in all this? In a word - drunk. My parents divorced when my twin brother and I were seven and later on - love my father though I did - and inspiring and sweet though he was in other ways - for the most part he was simply not around, or, when he was, only to be found proverbially drowning his sorrows in a bottle of whisky.

A successful documentary filmmaker in the 60s (his film 'Snow' was Oscar-nominated in 1964), he retreated into drink when a combination of new technology and his own rigid communist principles conspired to make him redundant in a highly commercial market, more or less from his mid-thirties to the end of his effective working life. Subsequently, whenever I would try and talk to him about my mother's BPAD extremes, he would react like a Dickensian character and, clutching his whisky glass, all but raise his other hand melodramatically to his brow declaring how living with her had wounded him far too much to discuss it.

IV

However, the child of a BPAD parent very definitely *does* have to discuss it. In this context, *Burnt Dress* can be viewed as a retrospective dialogue detailing how, by early adolescence, I found that I had become a confusing mix of my mother's mental nurse, whipping boy, prisoner, confidante, social worker and skivvy: true of all children to an extent, no doubt, but not, I think, in such an extreme way.

Santayana famously observed 'those who cannot remember the past are condemned to repeat it.' In this respect, one controversial aspect of BPAD is its capacity to transfer to the next generation, with one family sometimes manifesting successive sufferers. The aetiology of this syndrome is complex and much debated. One side of the argument insists on an exclusively genetic predisposition passed on in our DNA. This scientific-materialist view has settled on a causality of manic-depression stemming solely from an inherited (DNA-programmed) dysfunction of one or two kinds: either a faulty, in some way impaired neuronal connection in the brain, or a chemical imbalance that affects the sufferer's overall nervous system. The claim is that either of these physical dysfunctions – or perhaps both together - lead to the violent mood swings now known as bipolar affective disorder.

Conversely, psychoanalytical research, of course, favours an aetiology rooting BPAD in dysfunctional mental attitudes and emotional complexes, which, unresolved, lead to dangerous neurosis. It is important to add that the psychiatric approach does not entirely rule out a chemico-neurological element in BPAD, but is of the (general) opinion that where any chemical imbalance may, in certain cases, be found to exist in BP sufferers, this, too, has *its source in prolonged and repeated moods of repressed anger and deep frustration,* which themselves over time, and through the mechanism of the nervous system, trigger a toxic synthesis of chemicals, thus creating the environment for rapidly changing, extreme mood swings.

Again, in contrast, and in support of their approach, the scientific-materialist community often highlight the effective use of various drugs to control the effects of BPAD. Insodoing, they adduce that the efficacy of drugs such as Lithium prove that this mental affliction has its roots in the body and not the mind. However, as someone who has lived intimately with a BPAD sufferer – and also known several others – my own observation leads to a different deduction: whilst I concede that the drugs may well work to suppress and contain the BPAD sufferer's psychotic energy levels and mood swings, I would argue that they do not cure the condition itself, which remains dangerously 'under wraps', so to speak, and is thus always ready to re-emerge, triggered by certain circumstances. In this respect, I personally regard drugs as little more than chemical strait-jackets which subdue the patient. What this, of course, leads to is an individual who is, in a sense, sleep-walking through their lives; one who cannot, because of the drug suppressant, ever fully know who they are and why they feel what they feel. In my opinion and observational experience, anti-depressants such as Prozac work in a similar fashion. In constricting the sufferer's emotional wave band, so to speak, they leave individuals with an increased sense of calm, certainly, but at the very real cost of a vital degree of emotional fluency and articulacy. A friend briefly on Prozac during a difficult period once told me he didn't feel so depressed, certainly, but, conversely, he didn't real feel anything much at all! Being on Prozac was, for him, like being in an emotional limbo where nothing seemed real and no conclusions could be drawn about experience! He occupied a position of emotional neutrality in which his days slipped by meaninglessly.

However, I do not want to overstate my position in respect of the proper uses of pharmacological aids in the case of a BPAD sufferer. In my opinion, there may well be times, for example, when the drugs are absolutely necessary to calm down an actively schizoid patient. One of the awful effects of madness (that word!) is that, in its wake, it ushers in terrifying physical forces. These cannot be ignored. They must be restrained for the well-being of all concerned. If drugs can help here temporarily, then so be it – and with gratitude, again, to all concerned!

Here, I would also gladly observe that on a certain obvious level, it would be foolish (and indeed, unimaginative) to deny the essentially dynamic nature of the mind-body relationship, not just in BPAD sufferers, but in us all: to take only the most obvious examples: nervousness that induces dryness in the mouth; prolonged stress a headache; or most extreme of all: the catastrophic emotional shock that stops the heart.

However, as mentioned earlier, far from negating it, this mind-body connection seems to me to support psychoanalytical psychiatry's claims that the roots of BPAD are to be traced back to the mind, and that the effects are then passed back into the body. Again, my own experience and perception would seem to confirm this psychoanalytical aetiology of manic depression, i.e., that what is passed on in families is actually the emotional dysfunction and abuse, whereby one generation's cruelty is transferred to, and implanted in, another's consciousness, the extreme patterns of BPAD thus being tragically replicated ad infinitum.

In this regard then (and to my mind), Freud surely unveiled a profound truth when he analysed that most 'acausal' depression with no obvious external source in, say, personal, financial or career misfortunes or serious illness and bereavement, etc, usually has its root in repressed anger, i.e., rage which has been unconsciously deflected from its proper target (in my mother's case, her abusive parent), only to be disastrously redirected against oneself in the form of depression. In this respect - and to break the chain - I would aver that before they themselves become parents it is crucial that those who have suffered psychologically abusive upbringings come to some kind of consciousness about the exact nature of their own disturbed childhoods. Failure to do so will inevitably result in them tragically repeating the destructive pattern of depression and anger in the context of their own parent-child relationships. There is also a danger that those who adopt an exclusively scientific-materialist aetiology of BPAD will consciously ignore any experience of the so-called 'talking cure,' which psychoanalysis offers. This will, in my opinion, entrain serious ill-effects for both the sufferer and his/her dependants.

There is, it is crystal clear, much to learn in this sphere. Fortunately, we now live in an age when discussion and investigation of mental illness is no longer frowned upon. Major research now goes on into BPAD and there has been an attendant change in popular attitudes to this much-misunderstood mental illness. In these, the actual and metaphorical early days of a new century, there is (or so it is at least claimed) a much greater willingness to face the reality of psychosis and to accept that its incidence in society is much greater than previously admitted. Concomitantly, there is, it is also asserted, far less stigma attached to the fact of mental illness and to those who suffer from it. If true, this is surely a good thing: few would argue that a truly civilised society will seek not to condemn the mentally ill, but to understand their suffering and try and alleviate it – we have come a long way from the rich paying to look and laugh at the inmates of Bedlam!

On the other hand, there is, in my opinion, a very real danger that we will stray too far in the opposite direction and, by over-rationalising the problem, try and mitigate its reality; perhaps even unconsciously attempt to 'explain away' the personal and social disaster that is psychosis in general and BPAD in particular; attempt, as it were, by means of a mixture of modern medical language and bourgeois diplomacy, almost to understate mental illness, if not out of semantic existence altogether, then certainly out of consideration as a potentially life-threatening disorder (which it very definitely can be, taking into account the statistics of suicides and homicides connected with pre-existent mental pathologies).

It is perhaps interesting in the above context to note that hardly ever these days do we describe someone suffering from mental illness as 'mad'. It is as if the simple Anglo-Saxon presents too plain and powerful a prospect for us to bear: conversely, we must dress the condition up in an alternative medical nomenclature. In this regard, I noted earlier our age's current preference for the emotionally neutral term BPAD as preferable to the far more poetic – and actually more descriptive term 'manic-depression.' I am sometimes compelled to question why we believe the severity of certain conditions will be diminished if we simply call them by another name? Perhaps such a belief bespeaks a covert understanding that language is actually a much more terrifyingly powerful tool than we care to realise; that perhaps language itself can, in certain circumstances kill or cure. But that, no doubt, is another story.

What is currently vital, it seems to me, is an awareness that in attempting to mitigate the severity of BPAD - however understandable such an attitude – there is a very real danger we will thus disallow ourselves an honest reaction to what is, after all, the horrifying reality of the acute form of this mental illness.

In this context – and I concede my observations in this respect are, of course, anecdotal - I detect in recent times an increasing desire in our media to imply that BPAD has now attained the status of a socially acceptable – even, dare we say it, in certain circles, 'vogue-ish' affliction. In this respect one hears of movie stars and other celebrities suddenly announcing, in the glamorous glare of flashlights, that they are bipolar and need some time away from publicity, etc, etc – almost as if the condition were akin to an alcohol or drug addiction; i.e., a chronic, but highly treatable disorder that, with slight adjustments made both by the sufferer and by society, will be shortly resolved and normal service swiftly resumed: a couple of weeks in rehab and away you go, so to speak!

The truth is, of course, that, as with all illnesses and diseases, there are degrees of severity thereof. The danger lies in banding all degrees of BPAD under one heading, so that the movie star enjoying a period of euphoria succeeded by a pronounced and, for him or her, prolonged sense of dejection is suddenly treated the same as a psychotically unhinged BPAD person whose very life is at risk from the condition. I must say that in this particular regard some members of the medical profession do society no favours in succumbing to what may be considered to be trends in diagnosis. At the risk of trivialising the context, it reminds me of an early (analogous) experience as a mother myself, when I took my, then, three-year-old son to the doctor with a persistent cough only to have him quickly diagnosed as asthmatic and sent away with a lifelong commitment to an inhaler! Needless to say, he got better a week later and never used the inhaler again.

I cite this banal analogy to support a serious point: that, like all fields of human endeavour, science itself is not immune to fashion and that professional diagnosis sometimes undergoes societal pressure, reacting with unhelpful swings this way and that.

In my personal experience as someone who has themselves suffered at the hands of a serious BPAD sufferer, it is vital for all involved to realise expressly that there exist degrees of depression, despondency and dejection, and that these cannot all be banded together under one umbrella term – however convenient that might be for society.

We can all experience quite pronounced mood swings of one kind or another during the course of any given week – or day: this does not make us bipolar. Nor is an adult 'tantrum', however undesirable and unusual, equivalent to an authentic psychotic episode. Indeed, in my opinion it does a great disservice to authentic BPAD sufferers – and to those people trying to help them – to band the former with the latter in one amorphous group.

Indeed, if one were being ungenerous here one might link such a careless diagnostic philosophy to the incidence of violent crimes, assaults and murders committed by individuals tragically and fatally deemed fit by authorities to be released back into the community – either to live unattended or to receive some vague notion of 'care in the community.'

Of course, each individual time-frame differs. Speaking personally, with specific regard to my early 20s, I used to be very angry about my mother's behaviour: I was frequently passionate and hopelessly voluble on the subject - apologies to those friends and acquaintances whose ears I bent all those years ago! It took a decade or so, and a highly influential relationship, before I felt I could effectively deal with this psychological complex in an objective way. Towards the end of that period, perhaps with strange synchronicity, my own thoughts began to turn to the prospect of being a mother myself.

Of course, once embraced, it is a commonplace that the early years of motherhood constitute a barely-regulated chaos. One has little time for anything except the ongoing, utterly daunting challenge of securing one's baby's general well-being and relative moment-by-moment happiness! Speaking personally, it was only when my son started full-time education that I found myself suddenly willing and able to turn back to my past and review it again in a deeper, critically cool, even-minded way. Perhaps I was provoked to do so because, as events transpired, my relationship with my own mother was still very difficult at that time, and I found myself still very much driven by the need to investigate this tempestuous relationship further, to resolve the issues that lay at its heart – and ultimately to write about the subject matter that became *Burnt Dress*. Insodoing I very definitely didn't want to

X

come across in any way as hysterical or martyred in its pages, neither of which I was.

Here, I ought to state a word or two by way of qualification. Self-pity is a repulsive trait in human nature. No doubt my own childhood was a long way from being the worst in the world. Setbacks, reversals and misfortunes hit everyone. No life, however seemingly charmed, remains untouched for long; nor despite an industry of books on the subject, is there such a thing as the perfect parent. To be human is, of course, to err and I have no doubt that one should forgive; what I do contest vigorously is that one should also forget. That way, it seems to me, the patterns of repeated mental cruelty lie.

As a book, then, Burnt Dress has, I hope, resonance not just for women, but for all those interested in the fate of a relationship as simultaneously quintessential and dysfunctional as the one between mother and daughter documented in these pages. More specifically, I hope the book may be especially helpful to the children of bipolar and mentally unstable parents, whatever their gender. In this connection I've been pleased to observe the evolution over the past decade of an area of study and research directly concerned with the experiences of those now termed 'bipolar offspring.' As a result, a body of literature now exists that depicts, details and scientifically dissects the vicissitudes endured by this hitherto ignored section of society.

Indeed, until this recent development I have felt that we were an entirely unsung and unrecognised group: not so abused that we are taken into care, but abandoned, nevertheless, in an emotionally unstable world that, from the outside, could look deceptively normal. This was perhaps especially true of us because my family was, to state the fact without equivocation, well-off - though I have no doubt the same applies to many other children from less financially privileged families. Ironically, I've observed the trivial truth that, like many matriarchs from the upper-middle class, my mother actually operated a markedly stingy domestic economy! Indeed, as if to prove her own credentials for thrift, and though this was the dawning era of the cheap 'package holiday', she pointedly only ever took us on one foreign holiday during our entire upbringing – Sussex and Cornwall being otherwise considered adequate for our childish sensibilities.

I'm not asking for sympathy - they are beautiful places – I just state this as a plain fact and a petty clue to the sort of upper-middle class monetary mind-set prevalent at the time, an attitude not simply attributable to the 'make-do-and-mend' resourcefulness and stoicism of those who lived through the second world war. However – and ironically – I must also add here that it has been noted that usually, where bipolar sufferers' attitudes to money are concerned, extravagant over-spending is the norm!

More seriously, it's important for me to say at this juncture that I'm not in any way unsympathetic to those who suffer from the dreadful, destructive condition of BPAD. That said, I do believe that the pool of many, if not most, depressives - manic or otherwise - largely draws its source from the pathologically entrenched attitudes of those who cannot, or will not, for whatever reasons, address, analyse - and thereby come to terms with - the psychological abuse perpetrated upon them in their own childhoods; the main reason being that to be honest about one's parents carries with it some very exposing implications. Rejecting their pathological treatment of one can, indeed, feel too akin to rejecting them as parents altogether. But I think I would have risked insanity myself had I not been able, with the help, as I say, of a crucial friendship, to analyse what had happened in childhood and teenagery.

The style of Burnt Dress

Though diverse in style, employing prose, playscript, poetry (and even a faux multiple-choice question paper), Burnt Dress tells a linear story that should, ideally, be read from beginning to end. The use of different styles came about naturally as an instinctive response mirroring the crazily alternating situations one found oneself in. The BP person can, for example, be tremendous fun as they climb up to an often vertiginous high, but once on one, their emotional tides can turn terrifyingly quickly and violently. Learning to deal with this as a child involved a degree of emotional   detachment.   Likewise,   certain pieces in Burnt Dress quite naturally assumed a satirical matter-of-factness; although I'm aware that they can seem almost cruelly detached at times. I felt it was my prerogative to bring humour into some of the pieces, thereby sanctioning it for the reader, which I hope

XII

is the intended effect! Black humour is a vital resource for a mind benighted by disquiet. Unleavened by it, someone else's psychosis can be a monotonously dark subject. Thus a couple of images in *Burnt Dress* itself are, I can say – with profound apologies to my own long-faded teenage angst – expressive of a sense of the absurd, even of the outright black comedy of some of the situations I found myself in.

Again, some of the latter are reflected in poems which may employ the simplest of rhyme schemes or sport a shamelessly limerick rhythm as the simple, technical counterparts to their almost 'throwaway' absurdity. Intentionally terse, I think the poems and verses in question carry more impact.

There is some quite steely stuff, too, which was my response to my mother's cruelty and it can come over as cruel itself: whilst I find my now distant emotions totally understandable, I'm surprised at how uncompromising they are. They were though, it must be said, about sheer survival. They stand for what they are and I still stand by them! I should add that reading Nietzsche's "Be careful when you fight monsters, lest you become one" had profound resonance for me – I knew I had to watch out.

Preparing this final draft, having completed a first draft seventeen years earlier and having then put it on an actual and metaphorical shelf (the priorities of motherhood, directing and teaching drama took over), I discovered large gaps in the time-line that I realised needed filling. Failure to do so would have seriously marred the coherence of the narrative strand that runs through *Burnt Dress*. So there are some retrospective pieces in the volume. In these, the portrait of my mother can still be stark but not, I feel, without reason. Conversely, still in this context, I feel it is very much worth declaring that a mutual affection and forgiveness is now the hallmark of our relationship, something I value beyond words.

I have held off the thought of publishing *Burnt Dress* for many years. Over the decades, I've come to realise that being taken away from our mother and put in care as young children would have been even more damaging to us than being left with her on our own. When she was sectioned in mental hospitals it was traumatising, when she came back it could be no less so, but I have the sense that losing her all together would have made redemption that much more unachievable.

What would really have come to our rescue as children was an environment in which my mother was allowed to stay in the family home *but with regular monitoring by medical experts/counsellors*. No doubt such an arrangement would have required careful planning then as now; indeed, where cash-strapped public services are concerned allocation of money and resources must always be a consideration. However, it is my contention that the price society has to pay in the form of treatment of successive generations of bipolar sufferers would still make such an analysis cost-effective in the long run – to use painfully fiscal terminology!

In summary, and to reiterate an earlier observation: have I forgiven my mother? Of course. Have I forgotten what happened? No, but the 'not-forgetting' has been captured, framed and, I hope, transfigured in this book, written many years after the events it catalogues, with as much aesthetic objectivity as I possess, and still, I'm glad to say, early enough in my life to allow me to move on from all the events, both psychological and physical, that happened so many years ago.

Jo Murphy, East Harting, West Sussex – 2018

Burnt Dress

I

Motherhood & Committal

PLAYGROUND TUG-OF-WAR

Autumn term, home-time, children scatter like leaves!
Strangely, mum calls us over to someone else's car,
Gripping our shoulders, glancing wildly around us,
Whispers: "Tea at a friend's today, it isn't very far."

Behind her, a favourite uncle screeches up in a taxi,
He calls us over but is drowned out by a scream,
Other families stare as mother storms towards him,
Scattering the 'Lady-Bird' book queue for ice-cream.

Shoved into the car, we're driven to the friend's house,
No-one has, as yet, explained anything to us.
The house is strange, we sit for ages in the sitting-room,
Tea and supper both forgotten in the chaos.

We loiter in a corner as the house falls silent,
There aren't any carpets and the colours seem wrong.
Waiting, shuffling, staring at the furniture,
Wondering where the next parent might be coming from.

Three men arrive, murmuring in the corridor.
We peer at them, unseen, with our door ajar:
They're asking mum to leave, like our uncle just before,
Patiently ushering her towards a waiting car.

But mother howls at them down the long dark hallway,
There's a scuffle and as a stranger tries to shut our door
My brother bites his hand - we race to the window:
Her fearful backward glance silences the traffic's roar.

VISITING A PARENT IN A MENTAL HOSPITAL

In the bedroom of a London house a father helps his three children to dress. Confused, he tries to right the concertinaed clothes, until he smiles and tells them they will do.

After a drive through the city, out across the suburbs, they arrive at a large house. Walking in, they pass an aquarium through which you can see the room beyond, where groups of people sit, quite still, around low tables, with eyes blank, yet watchful, like the fish.

After meeting their mother, who says a faint 'hello' and then falls silent, the children ask if they can go back to the aquarium. As they all stand gazing through the glass, their mother announces suddenly, in a voice still too soft to be familiar, that hidden in the large stone cave is a monstrous black creature who never comes out.

They then meet some of her friends, who look at them before turning dispassionately back to their dice and board-games, like fish gently displacing pebbles at the bottom of the tank.

Bedtime, in the large house, was six o'clock. 'Earlier than us!' remarked the children playfully.

Later, walking back to the car, one of them asked why their mother had to stay there, in that room.

"She has nightmares, but sometimes they carry on through the day," their father explained.

That seemed reasonable enough: it was a hospital for nightmares that came at the wrong time, with a monster in a fish tank, where the adults went to bed in darkened rooms, before the children.

Later on, as weeks went by, the children would get small presents, with short messages from their mother, written in long, thin letters of black felt pen, on strips of masking tape, stuck across slim, square Cigarillo tins, their secret contents secured with black gaffer tape; opening to reveal thrilling ranks of Smarties, glistening in perfect rows, with their reflections mirrored on the inside of the lid.

Sustained by these sporadic gifts throughout the weeks, I'd picture my mother in that dark room, carefully preparing them, keeping us linked together, until the day she could come home.

It took thirty years to dawn on me, one unsuspecting morning, reminiscing on that time, that not one of those enthralling, vivid tins - much less the messages on the masking tape – had ever come from her.

ZOO-TIME

Living near London zoo, at night, you could hear the lions roar.

At dawn, narcotically restored to her somnambulant maternal role, mother prowled the shadowy confines of our day - menacing the menagerie called home.

At dusk, as if to compensate for day's eerie quiet, the household came alive again: my brother had nightmares, saw hideous monkeys and bears in the curtains; awoke some nights whirling round and round on the landing carpet, arms outstretched, caught in some never-to-be-fathomed ritual, crying through a litany of unintelligible chanting, mouthed talismanically...

Crocodiles seethed at the base of the stairs, and also under the beds (never leave your arm hanging out!) - I knew of a tiger who paced around the attic, searching for a way down into the house at night. So the lions' caged, nocturnal outrage roared its way into our dreams, and though our carnival of animals had begun to emerge at night, we could not know how soon they would begin to stalk the more audacious ground of day.

FAIRGROUND

Fairground! Visiting grandparents on the outskirts of my mother's old home town. Brother and I sitting, one cold October afternoon, either side of her, on a towering, windswept Ferris-wheel. My mother recently discharged from hospital; only just delivered from her most recent attack of psychosis. Was this a healing, family day out? Whose choice the noisy, gaudy, predatory fair?

My grandmother watched as we swung out on our tilting bench, into the great revolving curve, before she let herself be pulled away by a younger grandchild yearning for goldfish.

We soared up to the wheel's full height, and stopped. Swaying gently above fairground, town, lake, fields, a low wind gusted at the rusty, painted struts, whilst other passengers got slowly on and off below.

Unfortunately, a creeping, nascent paranoia which had been stalking my poor manic mother, chose this moment to break out, brought on, no doubt, by an altitude too abruptly gained: glorious, excessive!

In its normal capacity the Ferris-wheel provides - with its graceful, open-aired ascendance to great height - various things: wonder, exhilaration, and, for some I suppose, at times, real fright. But not, I think, the horror of someone trying, suddenly, genuinely, frenziedly, to get off, right next to you, the chair lurching ever more dangerously, the three of you suspended at the very top.

Howling, weeping, rattling the catch - with all her strength my mother shook the slender, single bar, then - twisting round — (unbalancing the bench), she tried to reach some non-existent route for her descent.

5

Strange to feel our apparent source of shelter and security abandon us to a chaos of wild neglect; about to let herself, and us, fall into the giant spokes, (at some point later on its implications take effect).

As the wheel began to take us down again, she screamed at the operator to stop the machine, sitting in his kiosk, he looked out from under dark half-lidded eyes and turned away. The crowds, the grubby window, helped to distance him, and perhaps he thought, (if he bothered), that she was reliving the sort of adolescent fun which includes a lot of shrieking.

How tragi-comically the wheel took us back up as she wailed on. My brother, (on her other side), as part of feigned indifference, pointed out a spider making its precarious way along the shuddering bar.

Absurdly, I felt new alarm, (it lurched towards me), although I understood that, by comparison, this added fear was insignificant: eight-legged or two, the priority for us all was staying on the chair.

I scoured the longed-for ground beneath us: where had my grandmother gone? (Roamed off to some stall to let my sister win a goldfish in a plastic bag). Never having needed to talk someone out of committing an injurious act, (this was the first time),

I think, at seven or so, I must have presciently used the simple mantras of the mental nurse: "Don't worry, we'll soon be down, calm down, we'll soon get off, don't worry, please sit down, sit down." Though nothing filtered through. Eventually we all got off. I don't think much was said, but have an uncharacteristic memory of my mother's head leaning on her mother's shoulder, as we trailed back to the car. In what state we left the fairground, I forget. Neither do I remember any explanation, mitigation. The silence as we were driven home, profound. (As it turned out, a scarcely less adrenalin-fuelled life awaited us, on the ground.)

6

THE SWING

Father rigged up two huge rope swings, which he hung from the giant pear tree in the long, thin garden of our London house.

Hair,
     clothes,
          laughter
               streamed
                    out
                     as the air coursed
               through
          the channels
that we made!

The swings' expansive arc swept us high above the dark trees, the next-door neighbours' gardens, until, over successive walls on either side, we'd catch sight

of rows
     and rows
          of other lives
               lived out calmly,
          it would seem,
beside our own.

When the rope's great pendulum slowed down, we'd wait, stock-still, suspended over the patch of scuffed earth our feet had made, thoughtful with loss, hoping one of you would put aside some distant chore, and give us again that height, that light,

That strangely reassuring view.

DIED IN THE WOOL

It had a distinctive, disconcerting look:
Cut in the style of her familiar mood,
Hanging heavy on the hook,
Mother's favourite black coat seemed to be
The custodial armour of her pathology:
Glinting blue-green crow-feather colours,
Impenetrable, wiry stitches,
Curled in tight whirlpools of malevolence,
She'd put it on, and we would know
How she would feel -
How she would act -
The warp and weft of the coming day,
Texture of matted fur,
Don't ever touch it!
It separated us perfectly,
Predator and prey,
And when she put it on
The hours ahead decayed.

HELL-BENT ON HAPPINESS

On some days you would find yourself released
From the cycle of anger and despair:
When, suddenly freed from the man-hunt
Of your own soul, you'd take off in pursuit
Of yet more elusive prey: a creature

Whose lair you never could track down;
Whose habits you could not predict;
And today, though you don't dare admit it,
The quarry you have cornered is happiness.

Your children stare at this rare laughter,
Watch it streaming down your face,
Transfixed by its velocity, its tone:
Almost outraged by its loveliness.

We grin stupidly as it rings out over our heads,
Though it is beautiful, it goes on too long.
Our own hounds yearn to join your pack,
How we would love to let them go!

If only we could be quite sure
That you were coming back.

HOSPITALISED AGAIN

[Now a housing development, Halliwick Hospital at Colney Hatch (also site of the Friern Barnet Asylum), opened in 1958 with 145 beds. Frankly described as a 'neurosis' unit for the "less sick, socially superior and fringe patients", it closed in 1972. Friern Barnet closed much later and was said to have had the longest corridor of any building in the world – {from: Lost Hospitals of London}].

Leaving her beautiful, expansive, blue-stone Hampshire house in the South Downs, your mother swept out of her gravel drive in the Jag' to visit you. Arriving, she couldn't help but be shocked by the institution's utilitarian nature and also subtly resentful of you for involving the family in the whole ignominy of your breakdown.

After you showed her round your silent, anodyne ward, shared bathrooms and common rooms she sat with you for a while and then, without pretext or prior warning, calmly, almost balletically removed her pearls. When, sixty years later, I asked you what this signified, you said you had the sense she was... dismayed.

But was it that the pearls were as out of context as they could ever or would ever be? Almost obscene in their ornamental irrelevance? Was it an act of respect for you as she watched you guide her round the dreadful, banal place your mental state had brought you to?

She didn't stay long. - Left you standing in the entertainments room listening, rapt, to a breathy actress-patient who was playing the piano, Chopin maybe; some composer that you loved. And as you listened you stared out at the first signs of spring, trying to make itself felt in the blank stretch of barely-green grass and pale blue sky outside the hospital's common room window.

Looking at your tears the pianist-patient stopped and said: "I'm glad I made you cry..." - and then continued, one hand gracefully o'erleaping the other as it danced across the shining keys.

DAY RELEASE

Had you planned it – or did you, an expert in such things, just act on sudden impulse?

Somehow sneaking past the white-coated backs of orderlies, one day you escape the hospital silently; coatless in deep winter, in just a thin dress, carrying a little loose change.

Taking the tube, you catch a Waterloo train out into the countryside, then a taxi home. Knocking at the front door by the willow tree, your parents answer, shocked at your abrupt and under-dressed appearance. Your plea to see your children is quickly shoved aside,

"It would upset them - they've only just had to watch you go."

Staying in the house was also, of course, out of the question. You stand disarmed in silence – emotionally and mentally utterly dispossessed as your father makes a furious phone-call to the hospital. Arrangements are being made that conspicuously and expensively suit nobody.

A few minutes later your father resentfully drives you back across the night to Halliwick Hospital. The journey is embarrassingly long and silent, headlights striping the dark. In silent torment you gaze out at the impossible nearness of a beautifully incurious moon and dispassionate stars.

The orderlies are waiting, he drops you off and drives away.

PSYCHO

There you are: disturbing no-one, rooted to the spot on the institution's corporation-neat lawn; standing, minding your own business of being mad.

Suddenly, out of the corner of your eye, a figure is running towards you from a distance, followed by other figures in full flight (and not unpredictably, wearing white); the figure - you realise as it draws near - is that of your fellow-patient friend. A young man, also committed by his family. You hail him – and then glimpse he's got a knife.

You do nothing to protect yourself as he almost reaches you - blade raised, as if badly directed in some old film – and in true Hollywood style, they catch him just in time. As he is dragged away he fixes his tormented face on yours, mouthing silent messages.

A day or so later someone tells you 'He's been moved to Friern,' that asylum's name marbled with dread, indicated - as it always had for each mad, sad generation - long-term, endlessly extended incarceration.

But not for him.

A week or two later it came up in haphazard conversation - maybe half-overheard, half-intended for your ears - that your friend had not failed to find another blade, and so lay stretched out on his cold, vitreous bed - haloed by the clinical glare of the asylum's over-lit, hygienically unimpeachable, concertedly unholy mortuary.

THE HORSE

At Halliwick, no doubt well meant, they built a gym for those in mental torment to keep fit for the duration of their incarceration (visitors never saw anybody in it).

There was also an Art Room, the pictures drying round the wall were dark, deranged and aching, like an exhibition by an unskilled Francis Bacon. From this Art Room, my young mother took a roll of white paper, black ink and a large match-box into the deserted gym.

She threw the roll along the room's capacious wooden floor, to echoes from the laddered walls; dipped the matchbox into the ink and printed out an image of a great, black, horse. A rampant creature, in full flight, clearing great space in one leap! Sacred image, one that I will always guard and keep. And when I think of that young woman painting there alone, make no mistake: I weep, I weep. I weep.

ZEBRA-CROSSING

Mother home again, it's time to do the weekly shop – drugged up to the nines, post-ECT, she drags us out of the house. Wheeling my scooter past the fishmonger's, I stop to gaze in at the off-licence - what sweet little coloured bottles! Count about ten, doll-size: "Come and see--!" Look up to find myself abandoned, the family prematurely gone; experience the horrible irrelevance of strangers' legs obscuring my view up the pavement. Desperately, I scan the far side of the street, and spot mother and siblings drifting over the zebra-crossing through the crowds – wholly unconscious of my absence.

I rush out into the road, dragging the scooter in my wake, denting the yellow footplate, (sending small sparks over the tarmac), straight into the path of a white sports-car, myself and motor screaming to a halt in a pall of acrid tyre smoke - the driver standing at the steering-wheel as if in a speed-boat, staring at me wild-eyed above his low windscreen, pale as his sleek car - the street completely still.

Transfixed by near-calamity, the shoppers glared, time froze, I threaded through communal indignation's glacial corridors and found my way to you: under-went the ritual sting of your rebuke, your fearful, angry face making mine pulsate with shame and tears, (that, and the people staring). But then the tableau stirred, the crowds moved on, the contours of the day swiftly re-drawn, just our walk home ahead.

Leaving the shopping bags beside the door, you took us three, still in our coats, to sit in the nursery; your arms around us, (rough sleeves upon our cheeks), calmed us with litanies of regret, hummed stray notes from long-forgotten tunes, watched the slow, grey city light edge across the windows of our basement room.

SAFETY-CATCH – (or, NEARLY KILLING MY SISTER)

Arriving one morning at the bank already in a bad mood – why wouldn't you be with three bored kids in tow! - mother jerked my sister's pram into its parking bay upon a precarious, sloping concrete slab – (in our childish way we'd already sensed the gradient of the day ahead was steep). And so I received my orders.

"Guard the pram!" my mother barked as she trod down the pram's ungainly foot-brake and took my brother in.

Of course. immediately listless I began to fiddle with the pram, first with the fringe along the hood, then with its rusting metal hinge: how did it collapse..? Maybe not. OK, then let's jog my sister to and fro, the London traffic roaring only ten feet or so below upon the bottle-necked road that syphoned the traffic serpent out towards the West...

- And so, inevitably, I turned to the brake with idle interest.

With one accidentally accurate click of my red shoes I undid my mother's work - the spring recoiled, the handle shuddered, the brake flicked off obediently!

Panicked, I flipped the bar again - On? Off? On? - Tiring of my indecision, the pram rolled slowly down the slope.

My sister smiled at the sudden speed; aghast, I watched her roll away, saw her decide that tears would be more apposite, her face imploding just as the pram lurched off the kerb, the oncoming car too late to stop---but then, as if making a leisurely choice of underwear from a shelf at waist height, a be-suited passer-by reached out and grabbed the pram.

He wheeled my bawling sister back up to where I stood, put on the brake, said something cautionary I couldn't catch, and left. Traipsing out of the bank, my brother glared - so he *had* seen!

But he'd have told my mother... - I was <u>sure</u> he'd seen. I started feeling waves of a new inversely thrilling dark emotion — the spirit of guilt! - finding itself at home and making preparations for a long stay in the recesses of my conscience.

Of course, I'd never have had a life if my sister had lost hers and for years I couldn't think of the pram, or its contents, beyond that moment when it tilted off the pavement. Later, in severely censored flashbacks, I dared to set the scene, in the chaos I'd glimpse my mother's demented grief over the small frame, imagine myself utterly eclipsed, cowering in deep shadows, deservedly dead to all, shamed into oblivion - certain people trying to be kind, (after all, I was so young), but no-one ever really able to forget the enormity of my deed, forever unspoken but always in the air.

But, as it was, my mother never knew. "Have you been fiddling with it?" was all she said on exiting the bank, (the pram's position was somewhat askew). "No," I said, heart ricocheting beneath my coat: and deep within my darkness, guilt gloated like a toad.

SPIKE

Decamping from the scene of near disaster to the calm of the fishmongers - last on mother's shopping list.

In its cool, dim, acceptably foul-smelling light, the old proprietor, swathed, remote and kind, in his white apron, gazed down and closed the deal with mother by handing each of us a biscuit, which we held up to each other silently, to acknowledge the cobbled surface of this unexpected treat.

As we shuffled about waiting for mother my red shoes made trenches in the sawdust on the floor.

A fishmongers is a place of casual aberrations. At first I stared at the glassy-eyed fish arrayed in shock along their icy, marble-slab shore; but what transfixed me even longer was the cashier incarcerated in her wooden kiosk – what had she done to earn such isolation? Was she the punisher or punishment? Who was she, this strange occupant dispassionately stamping invoices and impaling white bills on her monstrous metal spike! And then, as if mysteriously apprised of childish prying eyes she stopped and looked up at me... and in that gaze....

In that gaze....

DIVORCE

Some parents say it, some don't. The heart of what mine said to me was this: "Roads lead out across this barren landscape which we will take separately. One day, looking back, you'll see that certain things have been restored. Until then we'll work to keep our fractured lives as constant as we can."

Some parents remain friends, some don't. To some children I found I had become interesting – back then divorce still possessed the power of novelty. For other children I was considered dangerous - as if I had ventured somewhere forbidden, alone. A place whose language was the loss of certainty and security, the roof that parents held aloft, (we'd hardly noticed it before, not needing to), their carefree reliance, as they lay outside together, brushing you away - (like some annoying fly) - laughing, on lazy afternoons - you, playing in their peaceful shadow. And then the hollow sense that <u>one</u> of them, alone, could not keep night-fears away.

Much later, looking down from time's high ground, I discerned the roads that had run through fields, darting through cities and their desecrated limits, bridging rivers, winding through the woods I'd come to know too well, until at last I found one road wound all the way - to me.

Reluctantly I came to see that weakness co-exists with strength; that hearts might sleep a hundred years before revealing secrets (and perhaps not even then); that the forces of change, like river rapids coursing onward, still come to rest occasionally! And I would wonder if life was ever, really, simple, even for the very young.

Later still, happiness returned, unexpectedly, gradually, like summer's first uncertain heat: the slow awareness that the gradient was less steep, the heart less racked; the sense that darkness would recede: the knowledge that the sun still warmed us, as we grieved.

FORBIDDEN ARCHIVE

To My Mother

Where did you lose yourself?
Returning home on the hay-cart, with the farmhands,
Watching the hooves of the weary shires
Stirring the chalk-dust, releasing the scent of camomile
Over the long, dry paths of the downs?

Where did you lose yourself?
Listening to the rain sweep over the barn's corrugated roof,
Secure within its high cathedral walls,
Or drifting in the hop-kiln's resinous perfume,
Green garlands strung, like river weeds, above your head?

Where did you lose yourself?
Taking a short cut across the stubble fields,
White scratches scoring brown legs
Rustling through the sharp stalks, arriving home
To hesitate at the edge of the gravel's perfect shore?

Where did you lose yourself?
Swinging each black chain on the neat white posts
Bordering the blank, calm sea of grass,
Threading your way to the front door through the branches
Of the old willow, weeping eternally over its own shadow?

Where did you lose yourself?
Tearing off the stifling gown you wore
At the debutantes' last summer ball,
Snatching scattered items off the floor
As that familiar step fell silent at your door?

Where did you lose yourself?
Surrendering to her fraught cadences and fixed ideas,
Lying awake, as passive as the midnight lawn,
Your soul the willow tree, your mother's
Posts and chains ranged neatly round?

Where did you lose yourself?
Years of hospitals, committal and discharge,
Returning home, clinically deprived of memory.
When, now, they hear your distant step along the hall,
Your children leave their games:
It is, of course, their turn, to learn to dread your call.

2

Growing up in the asylum

ESTATE AGENT'S BLURB

Up for sale, our house:
Four floors of self-contained despair,
Adults on the middle two,
Children in the basement nursery,
Lonely au pair in the attic.
Measured in units of unhappiness
This house is worth millions.

Mere walls cannot relate
To subsequent inhabitants
The history of mother's labyrinthine misery:
Will the estate agent tell how,
Cerebral circuits jolting with ECT voltage,
She'd lose the way to her own kitchen?
Will he itemise the moments
When her paranoia soared and plunged
And she raged for hours in basement and attic?

Ah, that house. I recall the immaculate deception
Of its white facade, and the matching children
Trotting, in tightly buttoned coats,
To and fro over its threshold.
Of course, the estate agent's blurb
Will depart from these facts,
But why not exploit the selling points of truth?
Capitalise on the depths of her capacious sorrow,
The expanse of her uproarious mania?
One should make the most of one's assets,
And not every house has one mad, previous owner.

And what if we could replay the histories of everything that had happened in our houses? There'd be the achingly slow old-aged, drawn-out deaths, hypothermias, heart-attacks! And cancer's black flower blooming acridly in the vital organs of the old and young, (the body's profiteering land-lord: business ever booming). So, too, like hospital bed occupants tragicomically fast-forwarded, all the other illnesses would play out their ghastly repertoires as we, in sickly hues, red-faced, fat, thin, and coughing, paying out our deathly dues and with each rolling century, heading towards the corporation pyre or coffin.

Then there's the full panoply of sex: (no doubt performed in every room), homo and hetero and everything in between, seductive, sado-masochistic or more serene. Onanistic, solipsistic, the tantric devices of the 'mystic'. Cross-dressing and the bending of every gender, (for every decade a new permutation and new nomenclature 'LGBT+' our new umbrella combination).

There'd be household accidents traumatic and tame: Chaplinesque ladders breaking or unstable, an improvised chair tips off a table, the stretch from hand to light-bulb strung too high, angle-grinder cuts through bone and not the – obviously - intended stone and other fatal acts of DIY. Falls from windows, staircases and contortion after electric shocking; bulbous flesh trapped by the bath's tin walls; old bones snapping, a bleeding hand fumbling for the light-switch, (blood-stains on the turquoise flocking).

Accidents pale beside crime's more distorted human hieroglyphics: and yet most of us still want to know the rapes and murders' vile specifics. Some murders inventive - DIY inspired? - others predictable: a knife, a gun, a killer hired. Arguments silenced that long-since spiralled out of all proportion, wife and husband battering gone too far, nocturnal garden burials, infanticides, and all the other 'cides,' the cack-handedly improvised home-abortion. Bribery and menace, other silences too viciously bought; violence on the one hand grave and on the other, just an afterthought.

And then, in more unspeakable gloom, other diabolical inventories loom. Abuses and neglect of young and old. Idle cruelties, mental torture, cursory, cold exchanges, misdemeanours repeated by the habitually bad and perhaps as frequently, the unpredictable, wild excesses of the mad. Then just the familiar and banal: old and new types of drug, alcohol and good old nicotine: habits desultory and/or crude; loneliness, the memory's slow decline, divorce, unsuccessful adoptions, cheap wine and burnt food: survival's hard yards: sheer struggle or mere muddle in the hinterlands of time.

And there'd be much, no doubt, to enchant: celebrations, parties, flirtations, long week-end meals stretching over afternoons, home-births and birthdays, pet dogs and cats and budgerigars, sleep-overs, affection, children's ingenuity and invention; open fires, music, humour, playfulness, generosity, breakfasts, meals on laps, radio, phonograph, turn-tables and telly, DVD's and rapt attention, laughter, vigils, redecoration, improvements and all the stuff I haven't listed (including things too dull to mention).

Doubtless we should be thankful we can't review the delights or diabolisms of each home's human history, as, everlastingly, we re-create the stage-sets of our lives anew. Blank out the body hanging from the rafter and pursue the myriad things that we all do and, until the day fades on our own geriatric and increasingly sporadic laughter – perpetuate, on denial's gentle shores, the age-old myth of Happy. Ever. After.

HOUSE-HUNTING

Attracted by the ancestral name, mother saw the "The Old Curate's House," and decided to buy: "I can sense the mood of a house, the second I cross the threshold, I can tell immediately if it's haunted, or sinister in any way...." Odd then, to overlook the fact that the place had also been the village mortuary.

Of course, we nodded in agreement at the time, not caring, particularly, either way, (it never paid to contradict you, we had long ceased to challenge the remarks you made). When you told us the name, in my mind I drew the letters in colours of verdigris or light mildew. And the place seemed hospitable enough.

But then, not long after we had all moved in, your own familiar, paranormal restlessness set in. At night, having made sure sleeping pills had put the rest of you clean out, the rest of us would lie stark staringly awake...imagining we heard noises from the cold sunken room at the end of the house, once used for 'laying out,' and now our spacious nursery...

Could there be a lifeless body naked on the table awaiting the perfunctory rituals of its last, mysterious needs? Was there a lightly-rouged corpse lying in a padded box, smelling of talc, smart in Sunday-best, contemplating one last stroll..?

Or was it your wakeful psyche that haunted the corridors, making things move kinetically, taking its turbulent course down through the house? So convenient, this way you felt yourself in tune with the auras of the places that you chose: out cold yourself (yet rising with the lark), the only one amongst us who could not see in the dark.

NEW HOUSE, NEW HUSBAND

New house, new husband!

Still only eight, I sensed my new stepfather's main limitations instantly: buck-teeth, a bit dim, no chin. Worst of all, she didn't love him.

He was a sacrificial gift to her parents; his toothy, grinning head served up on a silver salver: conservative, cravat-wearing simpleton ("Oh, why couldn't she have married him *in the first place?*" her parents predictably enthused.)

I said, like some forlorn orphan in a bad musical — "Will I have to call him Daddy?"

— as if that would make any difference in the long run.

FALL FROM A WINDOW

Playing in the garden, bored, one beautiful summer day, age nine. Adults dozing somewhere in the indoor shade, had an idea to dramatise the afternoon: sister to stand at a top floor window and shout "Help!"

Then I would yell a long diminuendo from below, sister to send a heavy cushion thudding down into the garden, I would then hide the cushion in a bush, lie spread-eagled on the grass outside, and wait.

It all went perfectly, terrifyingly well: our new stepfather ran out into the garden first, then mother, screaming "Oh my god...!" upon his heels. Frightened by the horror in her voice, I scrambled to my feet and assured them casually it was a game and that we hadn't meant to upset them in the least.

They told me off and went inside, satisfied that we'd been playing out some imaginary incident (silly girls), quite unaware that others, in the house, might hear...

My pounding heart sent a potent mix of guilt, remorse and shock around my veins: why had I felt the need to confront her with a vision of my death? To test her love? Shock her out of this smug new marriage to a stranger?

But the terror in her eyes, when she ran out, revealed to me an underworld of loss no child was ever meant to see.

ISLAND PARADISE

With mother just over a breakdown,
Her quack recommended some sun:
It was time to fly South with the family
And fall in with all things Corsican.

But at our Mediterranean airport
Mother's equanimity abruptly unwound
As she counted the heads of her children:
Her young son nowhere to be found.

My brother had stayed on the airplane,
Encouraged by the kind-hearted crew
To explore the magical cockpit and see
What its boy-magnet gadgets could do.

In clouds of diesel and mimosa,
The last bus lurched off in the dust,
Whilst mother's wave of hysteria
Boiled over in psychotic distrust:

In the taxi, she was sure that the driver
Planned a family abduction en route:
He'd drive to a shack down an unbeaten track,
And line us all up to shoot.

At the holiday gates we swept in to a fanfare
Absently played by a three-man brass band
And like everything else, this limp welcome
Was listless, off-key and off-hand.

By brand name a Club-Mediterranean holiday,
With a currency of cheap coloured beads:
You slept in straw huts near the seashore,
And bored waiters ignored all your needs.

The wasps in the alfresco restaurant
Fought us for the food on each plate,
But with your mum in thrall to her neurons,
We couldn't care less what we ate.

My brother, upset and rebellious,
Leapt a-board a large fishing boat,
Paranoia set in – how long would it take
'Til a piratical crew slit his throat?

But he returned, taciturn, in the evening,
Mute as to how his time had been spent,
Instead hitting his sisters sequentially,
A gesture no less, in its way, eloquent.

The rigours of this gruesome holiday,
Denial has now succeeded in blocking:
But the straw huts were sandy and humid,
And the communal lavatories shocking.

One midnight, our, by now, mad mother,
Dashed relentlessly down to the sea,
And the only ones who could stop her,
Were my chinless step-dad and me.

She'd rave and sob twenty-four hourly:
Beyond reach of prescribed medication,
We'd nurse her through each new ordeal,
Racked by the fortnight's endless duration:

The island had but one remote hospital -
If committed, they'd confine her for years:
Step-dad warned she might *never* be free!
Were these his secret longings - or fears?

Mercifully the holiday drew to a close,
Departure came not a moment too soon:
We packed up our sand-filled possessions,
And welcomed sunrise on the pontoon.

On the aeroplane home she went barmy,
Ripping seat-belts off before landing,
Air-hostesses, drilled for flight-phobia,
Applied uniform, calm understanding.

So the return flight was not uneventful,
But safely boarding that plane was a thrill,
Heavenly islands are an infernal backdrop
When one's mother is mentally ill.

THE MEDICAL PROFESSION

Specialists huddle in groups like sportsmen,
Muttering stratagems in low voices -
Electrical equipment hangs on the walls
For easy access to their last resort.

On metal shelves stark with fluorescent light,
They register your extremes in neat files:
A gloved hand tracks alphabetical case-histories
And stops at yours.

Now, on the other side of time's library shelf,
I have tracked down my own imaginary files,
Haphazardly stacked, untended
In mildewed vaults marked "Childhood".

MANIC-DEPRESSION

When mother used to go manic,
She'd wake up at night around three,
When imperative work in the attic
Would transfix her all day until tea.

She'd hand-clip a hedge by moonlight,
If her neighbours had left it too long,
Reversing her car up their driveways,
With her badly-tuned radio full on.

There was nothing at all that could stop her
When that gleam crept into her eye,
She'd throw bricks through windows at random,
And seduce the odd passer-by.

She had various lovers and husbands
But they rarely tended to thrive;
Mantis-like she'd gnaw off their heads one by one,
And slowly devour them alive.

When she crashed from a high it was curious:
She seemed to lose all capacity to think,
Just sat in a chair, in drained, mute despair,
And for weeks wouldn't bathe, eat or drink.

There was no-one and no way to stop it,
At least that's what the doctors all said:
"But we'll give her some strong tranquilisers,
And stick electrodes onto her head..."

ECT left her timid, forgetful,
She'd lose her way round her own house:
"Could you tell me the way to my bedroom?"
So we'd lead her upstairs like a mouse.

Still the old spark could ignite any second,
One false step would trigger the switch:
A careless remark, a reaction unreckoned
Made her features darken and twitch.

Convinced that her anger was righteous,
The ends justifying the means -
Her holy war and revenge were religious
On heretics caught in their teens.

Children were mere lambs to be slaughtered:
The sacrifice spilled over the floor,
But if you're being hung, drawn and quartered
It's all the more hard to ignore.

Having gutted and burned us she'd glower,
Her impenitent expression wide-eyed,
As she hung up her psychic flame-thrower,
And stepped over the remains of the fried.

MURDER IN THE DARK

i

The second marriage went bad, the prospect was bleak,
My stepfather hen-pecked and ailing,
Their disharmony had, by now, reached a peak,
Each knew the whole thing was failing.

Stepfather decided that life could be calmer
If he did something she would approve:
He chose, then, the life of a gentleman farmer,
She sullenly agreed to an upmarket move:

An old farm was bought, renovation commenced,
And herds of new cows were christened,
Fields were re-claimed and smartly re-fenced
And the wheels of new tractors glistened.

Then suddenly, an entire year had passed,
So an informal dinner was planned,
To mark their dubious, gentrified status
On these acres of green, Hampshire land.

But in the elegant, draughty dining-room,
The guests only stiffened with dread,
As mother fired poisoned darts of disdain
Into our chinless stepfather's head.

She targeted him through all the three courses,
And made certain nothing went right,
(For she'd just fallen in love with the cowman
And yearned to abscond for the night).

ii

After the thin-lipped departure of guests (almost en masse), and a trying hour or so spent tidying up the mess, we decided, since the moon was high, to take a late-night stroll around the farm, to try and clear the wretched evening's acrid air: mother, step-dad, brother, sister and I, girls arm-in-arm, the men aloof, pet dachshund gaily bringing up the rear. Becalmed by a gentle late-evening breeze, and a billion stars in a sky of coal, we hoped their truce would last 'til bed, at least.

But we had overlooked the complication of the hole.

It was a narrow, deep and dangerous pit, next to the stables - (something to do with drains), its muddy walls were spiked with jagged pipes, mother thought a horse might wedge itself in it. So, seizing on the fact that she, her hapless husband and the horrid hole were ill-met in that moonlight there, she fixed him with an evil stare and took up the familiar, harping strain of her lament :

"A farmer should not leave a twenty foot deep open drain - it must be seen to - fill it with cement! Typical of you to leave it like that for so ludicrously long – don't you know? Can't you see - how absolutely lethal it could be?!"

How could she know she was about to find out for herself?

For, suddenly, step-dad tried to push her in: months of hectoring, lecturing and harangue had taken fatal toll of what was once, one must suppose, a man. Roaring hard, he struggled with the tangled threshing limbs of his now terror-struck tormentress, wrestling her to the slippery edge, whilst all around he heard us shout and yell, my brother pulling, lunging at his neck, my sister screaming on the spot, clinging to me (who just, I think, wailed on and on as well).

Then, suddenly aware that he'd betrayed the gentleman's status he'd won so hard (or perhaps simply concerned about arrest), stepfather lurched off down the yard bellowing mournful imprecations of despair.

Stunned, we picked our mother up, and dusted her down. She'd got a nasty gash the entire length of her back, (but it was only later that we were horrified by that).

Huddled together, dishevelled and confused, we went down to the paddock to catch our breath, attempt to reinstate a moment's peace; watch, in the rising moonlit mist, the horses graze; but then, bobbing happily under the barbed wire, our low-slung dachshund decided to explore: second, strange moment of alarm - our pony – (playfully? Maliciously? Sensing our dis-ease?) - starts pawing at the silly beast - bringing furious hooves within a whisker of the idiotic canine head! This starts the ensemble yelling off again. –'Til somehow, someone hauled the dog back underneath the fence, whilst another chased the equine fiend down half the field.

Nothing happening anywhere was making any sense. By now, in complete psychic disarray, we made our slow and hesitant way back up to the house, fearing step-dad had gone mad, fetched his gun, locked himself in, begun to wait for someone suitable to kill... but, instead, we found the house was still. So we went round fastening every catch on every door and window latch, and finally pitched camp in mother's room.

In fact, that night, our brother slept across the bottom of the double bed - clutching the madman's new 12-bore. For what seemed a long, long time, we listened for his step, his anguished call; his imagined, demented progress down the hall. But the strain of our adventure gradually replaced our dread, and, one by one, uneasily - we fell asleep, instead.

ORANGE ROOM

In the new farm-house, I'd chosen orange for my colour scheme, I don't know why - (my sister chose lime green). On late summer afternoons, the sun lit up each object as it passed across my walls of tangerine, taking its evening inventory of the room:

floral curtains,
matching bedspread,
mustard carpet,
my own private basin,
small desk,
chest of drawers,

the usual teenage stuff lay strewn about:

ornaments,
jewellery,
scarves,
clothes on chairs,

one or two favoured, worn, stuffed animals at the head of the bed as if comically marking the careless boundaries between childhood and teenagery.

Then I returned from school one day to find the room empty – no trace of me there anywhere - raided with deadly zeal, no sign of any occupant at all.

The vandalism was complete, the hoover's burnt rubber smell still lingering in the air – my erstwhile space now anodyne and chill, lacking only hotel sachets of sugar and shampoo, instructions on how to leave the room in case of fire. Perhaps there'd be a Bible in my old top drawer, and other information for my stay: was I aware of the shuttle bus to all the airport's terminals?

It was evident that I had left home suddenly without my own permission (it's true I had been flirting with premature departure).

Certainly, you acted as if I was, in some way, dead, or gone. Bristling with chemicals, you'd forayed in to fumigate the room, expunge all evidence of its current, or should I say, its former occupant.

The message as loud and clear as if it had been daubed in black paint across the walls: a silent, fastidious, and above all, faceless, ghost was welcome to book in again, at this tidy and well-ordered tomb; to do no more than gently stir the shifting particles of dust caught in the brief crepuscular light of the otherwise north-facing room.

NOT JANE EYRE

To Do:

Load the car with the following:
One bi-polar affective disorder person, known as "Mum"
One sister, Lily,12
Me, 15 and my back-pack
Their two overnight bags

Destination – 1) Howarth, Yorkshire. 2) My onward destination, Castle Douglas, Scotland

Theoretical Itinerary:

Travel to Yorkshire in high dudgeon, mother resenting the way I'd apparently 'gate-crashed my way into the trip' when she'd rather have taken her (favourite) daughter, my sister, on her own. Next: go and see the Brontë Parsonage Museum and then get a train the next day to a friend in Scotland, leaving sister and mother to drive home.

Actual Events:

Spent a long, fractious and rainy car journey listening to mother spouting embittered nothings about me, her life and other drivers. Arrive at Howarth and, instantly, we get on her nerves as we potter up the steep High Street: "Why don't you both use your initiative and leave me in PEACE!"

So we go and see the Brontë Parsonage on our own. Later, we find mother still browsing in shop windows up the High Street and, naturally, we enthuse about our visit. She is publically incandescent that we went there on our own, the whole purpose of our northward jaunt "But you told us to use our initiative – your very words! You were in a foul mood - what were we supposed to do?" we said.

Amidst the crowds, her black cannon swivelled on its mount and took its aim, and as unwitting day-trippers toiled by in cut-price raincoats blue and red, the battle lines were drawn. My own vocal ordnance curved into its new - and barely tried - trajectory - and it began.

She: I didn't want you on this bloody trip anyway, it was for ME and LILY – we wanted to see the parsonage ON OUR OWN!

Me: D'you think I enjoy being stuck in a car with you sniping at me all the way here? I only came because I had to get a lift half way!

She: Well now I've got you here you can bugger off to Scotland!

Me: Can't wait! And you don't own the bloody Brontës, you don't understand the first thing about them!

She: How dare you speak to me like that! - You purposely ruined EVERYTHING by going to the museum without me!

Me: YOU DIDN'T WANT OUR COMPANY – remember? We took the fucking INITIATIVE you're always nagging us about!

She: Don't swear like that in public!

Me: FUCK YOU AND FUCK THE PUBLIC!

And thus the invective flew: me in the centre of a rapidly widening circle of now transfixed rain-macs, (the tourists hadn't bargained for this, but why not? After the museum and tea-shops there wasn't much else to do, in Howarth in the rain). Mother swayed from right to left on the outside of the circle, (my sister half-hidden, more in embarrassment than fright), as the cannonade of vitriol rained down! The street lit up, the cobbles shone, the rain poured, the people shuddered, (with delight or the cold?) The victory, if victory it was, was mine.

Aglow with wrath I left early – and furiously - for Scotland but my friend told me, (I phoned to warn her), that she wouldn't be there until the next day. My triumphalism punctured, I had to stay overnight in Hebden Bridge, at a B & B with only a fiver. I ate and drank things I shouldn't, (crisps, half a tube of Nestlé's Milk and a miniature bottle of Advocaat, such is the indiscriminate and self-sabotaging nature of small moments of unpoliced rebellion).

The heat of the battle finally faded as I lay in that remote and unfamiliar room, forever, as it felt, at fault. But better that than the premature incarceration mother had casually planned for me inside our doomed, mad, family vault.

WEREWOLF IN PEARLS

[Entry in Wikipedia: "In Hungarian folk-lore, werewolves lived in the region of Transdanubia and it was thought that the ability to metamorphose into a wolf was obtained in infancy, after suffering abuse by parents, or by a curse or affliction caused by a bite or scratch from another werewolf]

Part I

Legend has it most werewolves shift their shapes at night but our mother could transmute throughout the day.

Certainly, sharing your home with a werewolf was both inconvenient and unpredictable. Trivial domestic incidents were bound to provoke the lycanthropic threat when sharp-toothed, matriarchal household standards simply were *not* met.

Examples of these might be inept folding, unmade beds or loading the wrong dish-washer powder. Beneath the over-shadowed brow the eyes begin it: irises churn, dilate and flicker from their darkening pit - an occult power undulates beneath the skin, as, feeling sicker, you watch her face distort and split. You know the rest: clothes tear, (your own, and hers), hair crackles into a wiry matted wig, a slavering lupine monster rips you to shreds with unsurgical skill. (Lycanthropy is, of course, itself, ironically, *so* untidy). Under the strain of one particularly bulging vein her necklace broke and pearls flew all around the kitchen, bobbing comically into corners as if at least *they* had their own will.

Part II

When the werewolf goes out (shopping or visiting friends, etc), it does highly authentic impressions of all, or some, of the following:

- ➢ Meekness
- ➢ Friendliness
- ➢ Conformity
- ➢ Tractability
- ➢ Humour
- ➢ And even, on occasions, good sense and practicality.

There are recommended cures for werewolves, these include:

- ❖ The piercing of hands, (bit brutal)
- ❖ Conversion to Christianity (debatable)
- ❖ The power of exhaustion (works on occasion)
- ❖ Striking of the forehead with knife (haven't tried)
- ❖ Addressing it three times by its Christian name (doesn't work)
- ❖ Scolding (futile)

Reconstituted after a lycanthropic day, (bones glued - flesh sewn back together any old way) 'normal life' would be resumed. An episode like this might conclude almost before it had begun, or it could run, and run, and run and run. Sometimes it exhausted her, but mostly it set her up for the day, she was somehow 'dusted down,' her appearance neat, each hair in place, and every pearl - miraculously - restrung.

BURNT DRESS

Ironing diligently, I accidentally burnt your favourite dress,
Scorched a large black hole straight through.
The treacherous thermostat gave up the ghost on me,
And not, (as fate had deviously decreed), on you.

Hysterically I cursed the still-smoking garment
And raced outside to shake it in a fury at the moon,
My brother kindly slapped me into coming to my senses.
Knowing mother would return from dining out all too soon,

I rushed to my bedroom, rammed the dress in a drawer,
There was no known way to escape my approaching fate;
I could have taken strychnine or jumped from a window,
(But I had notions of autonomy at some future date).

Next day she saw the damage to her lovely Laura Ashley;
Reality mutated as she stood there glazed with shock;
Inky clouds of rabid anger bloomed across her face insanely,
(So deep was her conviction that I'd meant to burn her frock).

As the work of the farmyard proceeded all around us
She ranted and she raved, with the cowman by her side,
I can't say that I relished being mauled like that in public,
(It undermined one's image and burgeoning teenage pride).

Many anxious days later, (having saved up for a tailor),
I returned the, by now, hated garment in pristine repair,
She glanced at the material and shoved the dress aside,
Returning to her housework with a curt, dismissive stare.

I burnt your dress while you were out,
Scorched a large black hole straight through,
And still, when I iron now, in clouds of spray and steam,
The figure who steps from the mist, is you.

MEETING OF MINDS

After yet another volcanic row the emotional lava cooled
And turned to stone along the flooded lane.
Still heated by the fire, I ran outside
To curse my mother in the vertical rain:

Out across the lower fields I called down
The storm's fierce censure: wrathful, cold.
We found ourselves of one accord,
Our meeting new, our kinship, old.

Wild with the storm's conviction, I returned
To find mother in an apron, wielding a broom
Brushing rising waters from the sodden ground,
Looking at me archly, through the gloom:

"Now that you've finished ranting lend a hand."
Silent but smiling I took up the hopeless chore,
Sweeping the water, and what remained of words,
In futile, steady strokes from the steps of the front door.

SHORT CHAPTER

Why we dared to go on holiday together,
I don't recall: just we two,
Mother and daughter.
We stayed in Bed and Breakfasts,
And wandered together,
Through a week of summer.

One afternoon, we sat in a clearing,
Along a rutted track,
By fields of wheat, hot, still,
The scent of camomile strong.
You read to me from Zola,
(Hardly a sunny tale).

We can hoard, if it helps,
The perfection of that day:
Its sudden gentleness:
Our deep affection unspoken,
Part of the heat-haze
And the silence.

STUKA

In this family war zone, the roads we wander are well-travelled.

Refugees in constant flight from your anger, we've learnt the sound of your approach, the verbal tenor of your mood, like the malign engine of a distant plane. Yes we know whenever you take to the skies, whatever the season; however brilliant the sun or stormy the weather, it's for one, and one only, ruthless reason.

Banking sharply left or right with violent speed, those of us left on the ground below can only marvel at your flight, until, of course, we realize that it's us again you have directly in your sights!

Loaded to the hilt with ammunition you cannot wait to use, you unload it on the innocents you habitually abuse – seeming not to realise this is 'friendly fire' upon your own people – or maybe you just despise them for the weakness of fleeing from the scene of their defeat. And so you strafe the road we're on: the very ones you should defend, upon whose daily love and loyalty you in fact, depend.

Vainglorious after you have landed, you thread through the dead and dying and find their melodrama trying. But all is fair in love and war.... And so the captive wounded stagger on, meanwhile, unable to reproach, reprove, respond in any way. Or are they...?

Looking back, it amazes me now that you could not see how your actions woke the spirit of revenge; could not sense rebellion stirring; could not see a day when another vicious plane would take to the skies, sinister engines whirring, the pilot's hand hovering above the instruments of your destruction, her own accipetral gaze calculated, cool – at last dispassionately unerring.

END OF LINE SALE

Shopping with mother: late teens, anything but solvent,
Yank the changing-room curtain just in time
To endure once again her ritual announcement:
"Of course I'll choose it, whilst the money's mine."

Furiously I haul myself into the material,
Criss-crossed with a pattern no fashion ever claimed:
Wartime utility meets Norland Nanny,
Who wants to wear this turquoise 'toilet-flush' shade?

Swipe back the curtain and parade in it sourly:
She murmurs approval and reaches for her bag.
So you like me to look frumpy and disconsolate -
Applaud the polyester collar and the overall sag?

You once slashed to shreds your own school uniform,
Got yourself expelled to shock your Ma and Pa;
But I've lost interest in the details of your tragedy,
I just don't want to turn into the monster that you are.

It seems, belatedly, you're trying to compensate:
And I'm actually being asked to conform for two.
Number these days quickly, make an announcement:
- Cast off on your own before the month is through.

WOMEN BEWARE WOMEN

Sisterhood, my arse! The very notion is a farce. Wholly and voluntarily obsessed with external appearances - no societal conditioning there! - my despotic grandmother, Kaye, who, in the legend of the day 'lived off the smell of a lettuce' had been outraged when she found her reckless teenage daughter - my mother Fran - escaping her rigorous dietary regime to, just occasionally, eat a cream-crammed bun between meals, in the local town.

Thereafter, Kaye made a habit which, today, may seem alarming, of substituting endless cigarettes for the fattening elements of her daughter's meals, (in the late, post-war 1940's, admittedly, this transaction was considered credible) and on she went tyrannizing my poor mother over all she ate - or even looked at - that was edible.

A decade or so later, when I was born, all fat and round, my horrified grandmother started early: "Aren't there 'Energen Rolls* for babies?"

You might think after a life-time of being shamed about her looks my mother would want to quote from different books: instil real values into her daughters rather than merely harp on about food-intake and weight - but you'd be wrong. The diet diatribe was, 'unto the seventh generation', duly handed on, along with added seasonings of guilt, blame, odious comparisons and lashings of self-hate. (Kaye had, by the way, her very own bipolar parent – an over-weight obsessively controlling termagant called Kate). And so – in handing on bunches of these frost-blackened flowers - witness how the female line empowers.

One summer's day in the late-70's swimming with family and friends in our haplessly tiny, bourgeois pool, I came in from the garden to help my mother wash up the tea. "Looking at you diving" she mused, her tone deadpan "I couldn't help thinking, with legs like those, you'll never find a man."

At sixteen or so I couldn't quite find an apposite retort to counter this point-blank poison dart and, anyway, still credulous and tractable, I probably, inwardly, agreed with her somewhat devastating prophecy. A wall of towering fury used to build when I dwelt too long on this small but deadly episode - but like all of us, with time, I've mellowed.

If I need to, I console myself by recalling how, later on and repeatedly, she would in turn, be vaporized by me.

* *Energen rolls were a slimming aid intended to be eaten instead of bread, made of an indigestible and dietetically questionable cellulose, now viewed as a wholly artificial substance.*

NIGHT EXIT

Sitting up in bed one rainy night, writing my diary by torchlight, I sensed my mother enter and approach the bedside. I didn't look up (she was still spoiling for a fight, having returned earlier, in uproar, from a long wet drive to nowhere, working up her grievances).

"Aren't you going to kiss your mother goodnight?"

Slowly, I raised my head and met her chill, psychotic glare with an impassive, insolent and unwavering stare.

The sting of that first - and only - slap, (not her usual style), sent an electrical charge much further than she intended it to go. My outrage, after yet another day charred by her wrath, discharged its energy into the room; belongings seemed to pack themselves, my sister tearfully begged me not to leave, but mother's abuse had alchemised within me, and so the door slammed shut:

> Midnight. The beatific, icy rain
> Extinguished, almost with a hiss,
> My anger's insurgent heat and flame
> And suddenly I was standing in the lane
> With a suitcase, silly teenage purse
> And ten pounds to my name.

In time the furnace of regret may refine what we feel,
Back then your phoned apology couldn't melt my new resolve:
I found the fire of your extremes had forged a certain steel
No future flame, however fierce, could ever, now, dissolve.

TABLES TURNED

In the record of our conflict, I recall the first time
I remained dry-eyed, cold, detached.
At first, you were astounded – our encounters
Usually followed plans you'd hatched.

In normal circumstances, my tears would signal
That you'd done what you'd set out to do:
Add new allegations to your dossier of disdain,
Convincing me each listed lie was true.

But, on this inaugural occasion, I felt your anxiety,
Fear - dare I say - terror, hiding, like a bird
Caught in the room; suddenly my power struck me:
I confess that exultation is too weak a word...

Of course, the skill eventually would be,
To judge the time to cast aside this hate,
And, for the sake of life, love and sanity:
Not to leave vital disarmament too late.

MAIDEN VOYAGE

So waking one morning from a nightmare - gasping, you could say, as I swam up from the bottom of sleep's ocean - I found I had sounded the depths of my hatred for you. Raising its anchor from the soul's sea-bed I also found a vessel ready to set sail.

That year the first page of my diary read like a ship's log in which I roughed out my motives for departure; wrote, in black ink, strong, bleak words to navigate where such feelings might lead; wrote like a cartographer intent on unknown seas; in short, I took up a mariner's skills.

Not, of course, that my prospective voyage met with your blessing. Observing signs of preparation, you'd seek absolution in a tide of tears. But, met by my silent resolution, these soon swelled over into all the usual angry storms. And yet, where once these would have capsized my craft, I found, however high your waves, the ship, at last, was worthy of the sea...

So, catching a fair wind after the storm, I ran my eye over mast and prow and without ceremony, cast off.

I can see you standing there - on my childhood's concrete quayside, gazing out to sea. Time after time you scoured the waves, but could not find me anywhere.

I'll send postcard sentiments from far away, and maybe I'll turn up one day; I'll keep on writing, anyway,

In the meantime - send good luck, and lots of love.

Take care.

3

Deliverance & Reconciliation

Staggered through a teaching degree! Four years at university: Education and Drama - swotted for and, by now, nearly won; jogging along with plodding, decent friends, (kept up over the years with none); learning about 'the development of the young child,' whilst still in the dark about myself; writing dissertations, enduring teaching practice, (the nursery kids were sweet but fractious, my colleagues either fierce or feeble); steering myself - quite open-eyed, yet, at the same time, all too tractably (was the fear) into a laced-up flat-shoed teaching career.

The high point was Hamlet, (drama was my major): corralled my lecturers into key parts, hired a vain actor-at-rest to play the Dane and filled in the rest with friends, (two Goths called John and Jane on Lighting) all of us storming an unwitting little theatre in the neighbouring college's attic: "Loove!? 'Is affeckshuns doo not that waay tend!" Claudius, (Lecturer of Art and a Yorkshireman to boot) would bellow. Had a fling with another stalwart Northern fellow, who, being Horatio both on and off the stage, nobly took the brunt of all that made me, in directorial terms, knock-kneed; but though a dear — if rather gruff - he was made of too, too solid stuff — and (no doubt I am myself too blunt) soon superseded.

Back at teaching practice in the nursery my very dear Froebelian lecturer was anything but cursory (his Teutonic perfectionism ironically learnt back in the Hitler Youth, and not abandoned with their dark uniform beliefs when he grew up and married a Brit): and this he counselled of the infants I was teaching:

"In trooz, you shouldn't ask zem to build bird's nests out of plasticine, zis is not vat zey have really <u>seen!</u> Zey should construct zem viz real tvigs: how vill zey <u>learn</u>, how vill zey <u>see</u> zat bird's nests are made viz bits of <u>zer tree</u>?"

And so the educational road ahead was nailed – or so I thought - thank god the blue-print was derailed: in an accidental rendezvous I momentously encountered…you…!

MAN AS COMPASS

So, up the stairs to prepare for my final year. September, a suitcase, books on education: study. An acquaintance's flat, share library time, get 'up to speed.' In short: start cramming. Instead, in a distant fragment of song on the stair and improbable drumsticks scaling up the bannisters you performed the fanfare of our future and bounded into view. Who the hell's this cocky fucker, dressed in summer blue seersucker? Blonde hair in flow, white shoes aglow, immediately and forever: witty, irreverent and clever.

Can't help but follow this comet and his trail: discard the drab, down-drag of doubters. Tell all my past instantly to this unlikely listener, oracle of contraries, slayer of the nay-saying, exuberant pied-piper - pinpointing, in thought and word both finely-drawn, all parental - and other - sins! This man, all stillness, all movement - hanging everything out to dry, airing laundry in public! Nailing colours to the mast! Again, weigh anchor but this time the ship's air-borne - look down, the past is suddenly very small, ignore the gradient's steep bend – who cares! – depart at speed – ascend!

NURSERY SCHOOL

So! College over, degree done, got what felt like the most minute job in the world at a Fulham nursery. Thirty children under four – a frantic and exhausting day with two helpers to assist in the affray: Beauty (Miss Edie Blessed) and the Beast (Mrs Ivy Battle).

Mrs Battle, professional harridan, was still fighting World War Two though it was actually 1981. Married to Sergeant Ernie Battle, (retired), domestic tasks in 'Battleville' had, before her nursery job, been regimented not to say cemented: Monday was baking, Wednesday laundry and housework on Friday, (front door-step scrubbed in the time-honoured working-woman's way).

Her orange lipstick went nicely with her short green cardigan and brown tweed skirt with matching brogues. Scuttering across the room, shrieking endless instructions to Edie and me, thus she had been steaming forth since Tobruk in '43. Smelling of starch and carbolic soap she'd wrench the children like rag-dolls off their chairs for 'toilet runs' - scything through their paint-and-scissored play until one day a child's head hit the corner of a table-top and bled.

(Her tragedy was, as in time we came to know, that she was mother of a mentally disabled boy, but we had a sense that other people's kids would always pay the price for this. Cruel as it sounds, she had to go).

Edie righted Ivy Battle's wrongs and together we lessened infant mortality with Elastoplast, a slower pace and the sudden grace of unexpected friendship and calm congeniality.

BLUE DRESS BIRTHDAY

"Don't look!" You steered me through the flat (and into the future). On the bed a cornflower-blue satin top, and matching pencil skirt, large ribbon at the back. Who was this for, this gorgeous cloth, this sensual attire: glorious paean to womanhood, draped across the bed yet rife with power, waiting to attain its siren shape? Where was this alluring 'she'? Who would be permitted such perfect expression of her femininity? The ravishing ensemble was, of course, for me…!

In the interests of truth, the skirt didn't quite fit but was exchanged for one in black velvet in which I looked, I feel I should say, no less 'soignée'. And when I wore it for some family throng how she kept sniping on and on:

- Where is that from?
- Since when…?
- What had got into me…?
- Isn't it a little OTT?

But she knew I was, to use an appropriately arcane verb, transmogrified: "transformed in a surprising or magical manner" – my former self having all but died, (except the good bits which remained inside). It irritated her more than she could explain to herself – or anybody else – and so confirmed to me, that fat, slim, clever or dim, I'd never her Jane Austen-style approval win, whatever shape, colour, warp or weft I ventured to turn up in.

EVENING INTERRUPTUS
(a play in two scenes)
CAST

JO – a young woman in her early twenties – (me)

JAMES – a young man in his early twenties – (you)

FRAN – Jo's mother, a middle-aged woman suffering from Bipolar Affective Disorder.

KENNETH – her lover, a well-meaning if ineffectual man with one completely stiff leg from wounds sustained in the Second World War. Sadly, his heroism does not extend to his relationship with Fran, in whose shadow he very much skulks.

Scene I

A sitting-room. Evening. All four are sitting watching the television. The occasion is supposed to be a sort of nostalgic event in which they are revisiting the scene of Kenneth's one, now long-gone showbiz triumph, a satirical British movie called "Dick" based on his novel of the same name. About a man who has a penis-transplant, the film was a success during the so-called 'swinging 60s', but has since limped into obscurity. The early part of the film is set in a hospital, with a series of pert nurses drifting to and fro across our TV screen.

FRAN: Oh for god's sake this is ridiculous rubbish!

JO: (warning) Ma…

FRAN: (aggressive) What!?

(Pause. The movie continues.)

FRAN (cont. *archly)* I suppose you had a riot with the nurses on set...!

KENNETH: Not really, Fran dear, I was just a back-room boy, really...

FRAN: Flirting with girls half your age —

KENNETH: They weren't actually...

FRAN: Weren't what?

KENNETH: Half my age --- at the time, I mean.

FRAN: And that made it all right!

JO: (placatory) – Ma, come on now...

KENNETH: (nervous) Honestly, Fran lovey, I hardly went on set ---

James looks nonplussed as the uncomfortable temperature in the sitting-room rises - as does the level of the nurses' innuendo with every successive frame of the movie.

FRAN: (getting up) I'm not going to sit here and watch this porn! Watching you sitting there... drooling over those tarts--! *(she storms out)*

KENNETH: Fran! Frannie darling! *(he turns the sound down, while, visually, in the movie, the nurses continue ministering flirtatiously on screen)* I don't know what's got into her – I thought she'd enjoy it – oh dear I'd no idea she'd respond like this – it wasn't like that at all, of course – she's got completely the wrong end of the stick - oh dear, I - I--

He freezes as he sees Fran returning. Framed in the doorway, she seems to have swollen to twice her normal size. She darts into the room to deliver an incoherent coup de grace.

FRAN: You and those... - nurses up to their CUNTS---!

Fran storms off again, this time with Kenneth in tow, trying to placate her up the corridor, "Frannie, Fran darling!" Their voices grow distant, a door slams. James stares at Jo agog with disbelief. There is muffled shouting from Fran's bedroom. Kenneth returns.

KENNETH: This is the end of the evening I'm afraid - she's absolutely beside herself, inconsolable. Um, I don't really know what to do. Er... I'll have to go back. Try and calm her down. It's really worrying – isn't it – when she gets the wrong end of the stick like this. Well, goodnight...I'm so sorry... really very sorry.

Jo and James murmur sympathetically. In spite of the inherent comedy of her insults, the atmosphere has grown extremely dark. Jo starts to tidy up the sitting room. In the background the TV images are still playing mutely.

JAMES: What are you doing?

JO: Tidying up the sitting room.

JAMES: Well what's happening...?

JO: What do you mean 'what's happening?' (Blasé) – Mum's gone mental.

JAMES: Shouldn't we do something?

JO: Such as?

JAMES Anything! I mean, what's she doing now?

JO: How should I know! …Killing Kenneth probably.

JAMES: Be serious. What does she normally do - when she gets like this?

JO: Storms around for a while… throws things…she'll calm down – eventually.

JAMES: So we just sit here.

JO: Unless there's anything else you want to do.

JAMES: What about 'leave'?!

JO: We can't leave.

JAMES: Why not? (*starts pacing around*)

JO: She'll be OK. She'll be fine in the morning. Well, not fine…

JAMES: Is this what it was like? In the past, I mean…

JO: (Dismissive) This is nothing. (*Finishes tidying up*) Let's go to bed. Unless you want to watch the rest of the film…?

JAMES: No I don't want to watch the rest of the bloody film! Fuck, the whole place feels possessed.

Pause.

JO: You get used to it. The pattern, I mean.

JAMES: You're sure we shouldn't just go…

JO: No. – She'll be all right. Her sleeping pills'll knock her out

63

[JO – cont.] - eventually. She probably won't remember anything in the morning…

Slow fade. The movie still playing mutely in the darkness. The VHS tape comes to an end and clicks off. Blackout

Scene 2

A bedroom in the house, half an hour later. It is now dark. Jo and James are in bed, their voices reduced to a sort of stage whisper.

JAMES: I can't sleep.

JO: Nor can I.

JAMES: I feel like the princes in the tower.

JO: I'll protect you.

JAMES: Shouldn't I be saying that to you?

A pause

It did have a kind of mad comedy to it though… That crazy sentence "Nurses up to their…--- "

JO: "Cunts".

JAMES: What was she thinking of?

JO: Their mini-skirts.

JAMES: I know, I know. But .. that sentence. - You know what was so weird about it?

JO: Apart from the obvious?

JAMES: It had no verb. "Nurses up to their cunts" has no verb. She didn't give it a verb.

JO: …least of her problems…

They share guilty laughter which fades. In the still house the silence is punctuated only by an owl's hoot and a vixen's cry.

END

RIDICULOUSLY ABRIDGED ADVENTURES

So is that it, I thought? For both of us? Me teaching myself to dreary drawn-out death in dingy nurseries, (no matter how sweet the children were or I tried to be to them!) You with your provincial newspaper hell-on-earth? Had we thus early drawn such blanks? No, what you said, you meant: let's go to Italy and see why Byron, Shelley and the others went, and so we duly did; only, I should add, with no blue blood and far less cash (mother swiftly called us 'brash').

Me: We're going to Italy.

Her: How long for?

Me: To live.

Her: For god's sake – when were you going to tell me?!

Me: I'm telling you now.

Her: Ridiculous! What will you survive on..?

Me: We're renting out our flat, we'll live off that.

Her: That won't be enough!

Pause

Me (aside) - Maybe not? Who knows? But then again, who cares!

φ

Upon what whim had the fates sent me down that long, contrived and unfamiliar route to Southfields and that drab flat in which we met? Sent us both, as it turned out, towards suns exterior and interior; towards poetry, passion, paintings, plays, sculpture, music, cities, journeys, a thousand teas, shared breakfasts, and above all – talk! - through, around, endless, fertile, futile, febrile and insouciant confabulation! Laughter outrageous! Across the sun-flowered continent, over Alpine rooftops and crucially, to Italy. Italy!

The only trouble was that mother too, had stowed away with me - or should I say migrated? Unwelcome and unsoutherly bird! Roosting in the branches of my mental family tree. Despite the distance I'd flown from you, you'd always reappear and perch upon my shoulder like a harpy, each day becoming bolder: whispering black doubts in my ear: what was I doing here?

Whatever I ate, whatever I'd wear, whatever I spent, whatever I did or didn't do, you popped up everywhere: ah, suddenly it was all so clear - I'd have to keep on murdering you until you ceased, necromantically, to reappear!

Italy! – eventually, as it transpired, five years rich in poetry's precipitous steeps and poverty's chasms, gliding down our local hill penniless and petrol-free in the blue, battered 2CV. Powered by the yellow light of sunflower fields – leaning into the toils of the Apennines, cooking pastasciutta grim and good, freezing villas, car-crashes and a snow-strewn return through silent France – back at last to Oxford's river flats, a rented cottage – and another country: parenthood.

ACRID

Prologue

Of all the subjects buried decades long, this is the hardest to disinter; I circle the memory like an unexploded bomb, the damn thing pulsing with undeserved shame, guilt and blame. I know I must diffuse it, because, embalmed like this, it will always have the power to maim.

φ

Pregnant: bit of a surprise, albeit a beautiful one. Penniless: more predictable. Two years after our return from Italy, me part-time teaching; man writing, doing odd jobs, making do. Four months into pregnancy and deeply worried... turn, fatally, to her. Arranged to meet for lunch in our old shopping town. She insisted on bringing Kenneth, too, which seemed odd to me, an incursion on the private nature of the meeting, but we were supplicants and therefore in no position to disagree.

But from the start it was clear that we had stepped into a small arena, we, the doomed bulls and you both matadors, adjusting cloaks, taking up your killing swords and banderillas. Pointed questions and sharp statements flew thick and fast throughout the opening of the meal – even Kenneth joining in with vindictive zeal, which was a little rich given his age and the times he'd cowered behind me, leaving me facing your bestial, 'hornéd' rage.

But that was then and this, no less bloodily, was now: first she addressing me, then him, and turning then to you:

"So what are you going to do about your finances?"

"Well...."

"Why do you think I should help when you've been careless with that money?"

"We haven't wasted it. It's given us the time to write, to ---

"But you haven't been published! Not even a commission!" observed Kenneth courageously, from behind her.

To which barb, a bitter, albeit still vulnerable silence seemed the sole dignified response. Mother, of course, filled in the gap…

"Perhaps it's time you gave up this writing thing and came back to the real world!?"

And then the lance's final plunge into my red, matted hide:

"And anyway what makes you think you're so bloody special?"

At that point, (though the main course was due – and large plates of pasta heaved into view) I decided it was time to go!

In an odd gesture, never repeated before or since, I drew the crisp, white napkin, shroud-like, over my soup: they'd spiked us both enough, the sand in the ring blood-red. But though our humiliation seemed complete, I sensed still worse remarks were coming to a head and I was damned if we were going to groan and die at their feet! Everything has a price, and my own bull-like pride was teetering – I'd go down fighting before I paid the moral bill this gory lunch was metering:

"We don't have to listen to this" I hissed and added vitriolically in your face, "especially when *you've* never earned a *penny* in your life!" Chairs scraped back, coats and bag snatched up, out we went, expressions daggered, my mother frozen, lover dumb-founded, waiters faltering, fellow restaurant diners staggered.

Out into the street, back to the car, "Drive off", I said, "before they follow…!" I felt horror-struck and hollow, but also jubilant somehow.

It was insane to sever blood-ties as I felt I'd done, to spurn that vital 'blood money' almost before the meeting had begun. I couldn't help but feel I'd done something very, very wrong — and yet her final reproachful words surged back in their embittered stream — the prospect of my having her only grandchild and being her eldest daughter were not enough, it seemed, to stop this much-revelled-in ritualistic slaughter.

REGAINING CONFIDENCE

In the lovely, unfamiliar hotel room,
I play a lady of means.
The white door shudders gently
To a late summer breeze I cannot feel;

I listen for the footfall
Of strangers in the corridor,
But hear nothing.
Thus cut adrift at last

From a legacy of bitterness and self-doubt,
I disinherit the worst of our shared past.
I know, in leaving you behind,
I end, within my soul, our troubled line.

So, for a while, I settle here, in a silence
Only September houseflies stir,
Warmed by the window-panes -
Have they been here all summer?

Outside, tall fields of maize shield the house:
With the dead tree
Standing gaunt amongst them,
They belong on some Tuscan hill,

And the white dirt-track
Should lead to vineyards.
So, too, rare English crickets chorus on into dusk,
And I reign here, over a new time.

PREGNANCY

Looking in the mirror, as I grew larger, so did my sense of doubt.

Like every woman, I contemplated my own fitness and capacity for motherhood and hoped the child inside me would never have to accuse me as I had done my mother; hoped that any instance of my own parental anger would be far less worthy of report, would arise only trivially to be forgotten in an instant; hoped that there would be no scaring or scarring him or her as she'd scared me - the very thought appalled: I imagined the sweet infant's face scouring mine in terror at my next move, dreading now, in turn, my step.

No, at home, at least, my child would never fear long winter grudges and disdain's unthawing frosts, but sense spring and summer lasting longer year on year. (A dream perhaps, since folk and fairy tales are full of tutelary violence to introduce the world's unkindness to children's unsuspecting ears: we know Red Riding Hood forever faces danger in the wood...)

And yet, in some echo of that same ideal world, we'd strive, in parenthood, to keep to certain well-worn paths, be pillars of strength, sheltering oak trees; lower the portcullis, flood the moat, provide large sofas and roaring fires and prove that inside our four walls it was secure and safe - and not patrolled by wolves.

ROPE-BRIDGE

Just back home from hospital - the gruesome tug-of-war of childbirth done - our baby son, beautiful but bewildering, lay sleeping fitfully swaddled in the midst of the obligatory domestic chaos. With the midwife long-gone, no money and one's mother nowhere in sight, I sighed to see my dear sister drive away and realise how deeply we were on our own.

Exhausted, penurious and fraught, I held my son close, perched it seemed, at times, as if on a rope-bridge of anxieties - the fibres of which frayed cartoon-like as I watched. Stupidly, from time to time, in an attempt to habituate myself to the terrain, I looked down at the abyss below and nearly lost my balance....

Well, time glosses over the past in the service of soft half-truth: memory has edited out the jagged heartache from our parenthood adventure, censored all our bloodiest anxieties. Suffice to say, like all new parents, we stumbled across the rope bridge of those early days - though it didn't particularly help one time when my brother reported how my mother had snorted from afar that 'babies don't need expensive cots or beds, they can sleep in a drawer quite comfortably...'

As it happened, that was the last advice or word I heard from her for two years - and so got on with my own version of what motherhood might be. When not abandoned to the solitary sense of my own intense inadequacy, this meant attending mothers' groups: meeting for tea-parties, afternoons sitting round, talking, consoling each other's real or imaginary deficiencies; comparing our babies' sleep and eating, contriving haphazard entertainments for unruly infants, playing, paddling, tripping, pushing, laughing, crying, spilling; dealing with vomit, piss and shit as if their lives depended on it – which, of course, they did.

Meanwhile, across the city, you worked part-time, wrote, brought back cheap food in a battered car, cooked and endearingly kept up the troupe's morale, whilst at night I disappeared into my infant's needs: dandling, soothing, winding and delivering those interminable breast feeds.

Now, looking back, of course, I wish I could reassure my former self that everything we did back then, would do; that the ragged bridge hung out across those first few years would hold; that we'd drive off anxiety's hyena as it scavenged across our territory each day and dogged our sense of 'getting through' – that we would even, eventually, reach a refuge overlooking an infinitely less fatal view.

But that's looking back.... At the time, the frayed rope bridge still swayed - whilst waiting at the other end was always - somehow inescapable, the black shadow of the 'anti-mother' that was you.

BORDER CONTROL

Yes, can I help you? Assist with your enquiries?
Where, exactly, would you like to begin?
Your letter declares you're my son's grandmother;
After a two-year silence, claim to be his kith and kin?

You ask me to inspect some faded snapshots,
Glance at memories your febrile hand once penned,
But I just can't place you, put you in any context,
So please, try to act on what I recommend:

The fact that I'm a mother now isn't your business -
I'll have to confirm you're who you say you are.
You'll have to leave your papers, if you want access -
Yes, I'm perfectly aware that you've had to come far.

And no, I don't intend to hurt, isolate or ignore you,
But I feel you may be barking up a leafless tree.
Come back tomorrow, I'll glance through the photos,
Research the person you call 'daughter' -

Somehow I doubt the trail will lead to me.

RECONCILIATION

It took a death to reunite us.

News came of a beloved grandfather's (my mother's father's) death, which, after our two year separation seemed, rightly or wrongly, to constitute some sort of hook for reconciliation.

First, you sent some family pictures of us all together at the various staging posts of family history; then the funeral's time and place - and another date to meet up, conciliatory, before that day.

I can still see your car arrive, hear the fatalistic crunch of tyre on gravel. Your perfume ever a reproach, your aura electric. Strangely, at this first meeting, my sweet, now two-year-old son hugged his grandmother as if in recognition, which was more than I could do. Though I sensed my son's need to know his 'other granny' (oh cosy soubriquet with hidden barbs!) Still, in some corner of my psyche I felt I had, for somewhat sentimental reasons, let her back into my life too soon - and on her terms, not mine. Somehow it seemed a capitulation and, after all the conflagration, more than somewhat lame.

Of course, things went okay on the day - albeit in that inevitably wooden post-feud way. As for the future: could we really find some simple language to 'get along' (surely neither of us could be so naive)?! In due time I discovered that, of course, in a kind of disabled way, we could.

Indeed, all too quickly, odd outings turned into more frequent meetings and then monthly get-togethers, until in time I dutifully went to grin and bear whole weekends at her house (pushing it a bit), to play the game and do the things grandchildren mostly enjoy – and so discovered for myself a brand new type of stress! – keeping an eye out for her behaviour towards him, whilst simultaneously overseeing his to her! Ensuring thank-you's had been said every two minutes; watching him having to listen attentively at all times to everyone and everything she chose to introduce him to – witness the Dickensian rebuke the poor boy got, aged six, for being bored by an old movie of Great Expectations that she, ironically 'Miss Haversham-esque' herself, decreed that he should see, only for him to point out to us ten minutes later that grandma herself had fallen asleep (we stifled laughter as the black and white images flickered on into the 19th century dusk).

FAIRGROUND REVISITED

Another fairground forty years on....

This time, on the local village green, it's me cast in the role of the mother gazing up at a Ferris Wheel – ruefully re-living the memory of my own childhood's fairground aberration!

Of course, our son and friend had raced to take their places in the queue for this minor view of heaven. And no sooner seen than sat in, the ungainly wheel duly hoisted them inexorably up into candy-floss clouds. I watched our boys imprisoned gleefully in the wheel's small, wire cage; seats rocking slightly to and fro – just enough to taunt the memory of that earlier alarm.

Unexceptionally, the Wheel performed its circular magic exactly as that venerable 19th century Yankee, Mr Ferris, intended it should do, and the boys sat quite calmly, peering down at paradise, looking out for other things they didn't want to miss, waving occasionally, sitting out long waits aloft, whilst other children clambered on, below. – Their ride over, we tried not to greet the boys as if they'd been to Mars, though, absurdly, of course, a parent is always relieved to have its off-spring – and their friend - back on terra firma.

There followed, with inevitable gritted teeth, a go on the bumper cars – them in one and us in another, pretending to be thrilled, though, in our own childhood days, we'd both hated the token steering and blunt violence.

Crouching low, as if hiding in giant shoes, the boys clung on; under spiteful blue sparks the boots began their imbecilic bludgeoning: I screamed as various tykes targeted our car and pounded us each time around.

Was it the crowd-pulling sound of female screams that made the youth in charge give us an extra go? Scrambling off at last, the boys, dry-eyed, relieved, grimaced at each other through pink strands of more candy-floss.

Eventually, I was relieved to usher them away to creaking swing boats and tacky stalls: 50p to knock down a fluorescent gonk, (using greasy, over-handled woollen balls).

Most of the small change gone and the stalls all tried, I looked at my watch, surely it was time to go? Our son was sulking, (goldfish and gonk had both eluded him) whilst, no less tryingly his friend made pedantically plain a marked preference for home, though his parents weren't expecting him for at least another hour, which, though irritating, was gloriously, reassuringly, bathetically banal.

BINGE

So the monthly visits to my mother's rolled by and as the years, too, revolved it was tacitly conceded that, overall, our visits, if often strained, had not caused too much mess – actual or emotional.

Both too brief and eternal, childhood flies by in the slow-motion bat of an all-seeing eye: I remember one of our last weekends with her, just before defiant teenagery kicked in and our son got too old to do the trip: things had been somewhat tense, with excessive checks on table-manners and strictures imposed on one-too-many cakes – so that when the moment came to leave, we did so barely masking a sense of liberation as we jumped triumphantly into our clapped-out open-top car in blazing sun – FREE AT LAST!

Stopping at the end of her road to fill up our tank, we also stocked up on several brands of sweets, then turned our favourite CD on and powered back home on the euphoria of being ourselves, intuiting that, at last, the challenge of the 'visiting Granny' era had been overcome – our freedom from that minor form of etiquette-torture finally - and forever - won!

MINDING THE BABY (a brief retrospective of motherhood)

Glancing, one day, at photos of my – by now teenage - son pinned on the board above my desk, I realised that, although I'd loved him no less deeply at that age, there were no shots there of him, as a baby.

Downstairs, of course, on mantelpieces, there are the obligatory showcase pictures dispersed to relatives: one shows him solemn, eighty if he's a day, (with his life still measurable in hours): gently swaddled and self-absorbed, looking back, perhaps across centuries - no sign of the incendiary device he really was, lying there absurdly quiescent in a lacy blanket (such are the short-lived dolls' games new mothers play).

Elsewhere about the house, later pictures show him laughing, playing, poking things with sticks - all the usual things. But for pictures from that earlier time I have to hunt in various drawers.

Of course, in babyhood, the camera is not fumbled for when one paces back and forth on sleepless nights, in a dark, cold room, on the edge of the world. Or when the endless crying fills a well of inadequacy with dread, or money worries elbow their way back into the foreground, or at the mock-altar of the nappy-change: - accoutrements laid out as if for some religious ritual.

Poring over several boxes, I sort through the sunlit images: there is the lovely child, and then, me: adoring, attentive, ever-present, which I was. But behind these dry-eyed, glossy shots lay a darker imperative that began to dominate each day:

Rarely asleep for long, (he'd never lie awake and coo), I'd soon feel the snake of panic rapidly uncoil - what could I find for him to do...?

Before long, every rattle and toy had been ransacked, all the spoils of this small world launched over the infant's shoulder: now a hunt was suddenly, crucially, relentlessly on, all day - and every day to come: a game where, month after month, everything in the house has already been hidden and found a thousand times, to shouts of glee (your own) - but still you must conduct a ceaseless search for things you do not want to find, over and over again - accompanied, at times, by someone crying...

On rainy days I'd take him round the house, ten, twenty, thirty times, so that his frighteningly enquiring gaze could take in this, and that and this, again.

I'd rig up hanging things for him to swat but both success and failure bored him, they were not, apparently, part of his mission. Desperately I'd cast around for new, safe home-made things, the properties of which he could break down: investigate, squeeze, pound, chew - destroy!

Eventually, of course, I forayed out and marvelled at certain other babies contentedly planted in one spot, playing with the same spit-soaked fabric brick for hours. I couldn't fuel the furnace of my child's unceasing curiosity: not hyperactive, he was merely on a quest...!

When did the sense of responsibility for his boredom lift? Perhaps when he could move about, or talk? Odd that I cannot, now, remember.

Later on, (whilst still importunate, as children are), he'd spend hours constructing, modifying, drawing, imagining, cutting, carving, sawing, sticking endless fragments of things onto other things until I've wondered how, in babyhood, with his blunt fists and pod-like frame he'd managed to arrive with expectations so absurdly disproportionate to his abilities!

He saw out there, it seemed, a world of waiting things just out of reach: craving a slide-rule he'd been handed a squeaking duck, (which, even then, he could not grasp). It was as if the gods had given him some vague yet vast, full-scale project in his head and vindictively left his body (sweet, stunted octopus), to do its slow, tortuous work of catching up.

So desperate to do anything to something, to grapple with the world by whatsoever means, he found himself with no real tools at all, least of all, the patience to wait the whole obstacle of infancy out until he could at last, begin.

And so, because the business of being a baby seemed to be for him (or was it me?) so hard, I find I have no pictures of him, in those days, pinned on the board above my desk, (although I'd loved him no less deeply, at that age).

GARDEN CENTRE

Reconciliation is a loaded word. But suddenly, a distance of two decades sets us at one remove from our battleground. The worst of hostilities over, on your visits now, we keep strict pace with the calendar: fetes or fairs in summer, in autumn, fireworks, and so on. In spring, we might go to a garden centre to peer at wooden racks of carefully grouped plants, and read the signs: some won't grow in certain soils, or endure too great a proximity to each other. We note that most, however, prefer sun all the time.

Not being a gardener, I always learn something new: did you know, for instance, that wind-damage can scorch your plants to death? The garden-centre has made its boundaries perfect, you know exactly where you are and you're given encouraging, if trite, examples of how your garden might look, with the right approach. (I like that pond).

Then we spin idly home, along the hedgerows, (I drive). Make tea, a meal, a fire, next day we walk, you talk and when you leave, we wave 'til you are out of sight.

As evening wears on, I file an entry in my memory (by and large, the same things re-appear each time).

On your visits all that matters now is that, for a while, we radiate a measured warmth; after all, these moments are too short for anything but sun. And should bad weather suddenly prevail, my roots descend too far to be dislodged by storm or wind.

If I find myself too long in shade, it's my affair; planting distance helps, of course, (I think a radius of a hundred miles sounds fair). Sometimes I hear your distant voice, telling me, as on these garden centre outings, about the sort of plants you think might flourish in my garden's altogether different earth.

I'll catch a stray remark, the tale-end of opinions, looking up, I'll see you, over there, moving along the potted plants' immaculate display, stopping to catch the perfume of some delicate, time-honoured favourite flower.

Our lives are perfect opposites in every way; your garden is a symbol of all you could not grow, your compost heap more representative in its decay. And though, against the odds, I flourish, in what ways, and how, you do not choose to know.

MULTIPLE CHOICE FOR THE MAD

It's taken me half a century to ask the following simple questions, and of course, they're all too late. My mother is too old to answer them now and I don't want to upset her shrinking world of TV, sleep and making tea, so the scribe who will complete this academic exercise on her behalf is me.

Question 1 - Why did you ignore the reality of our violent relationship?

Please put a tick in <u>one</u> of the following boxes:

a) I revelled in my pathological anger   ☑

b) I regarded it as wholly justified   ☑

c) Being mentally ill, I was psychotically self-obsessed   ☑

Question 2 – Why did you never consider the effect of your constant anger on me?

Please put a tick in <u>one</u> of the following boxes:

a) I had no concept of you as an individual   ☑

b) You deserved everything you got   ☑

c) I never considered the possibility of repercussions   ☑

Question 3 - Why did you deliberately stop, and never resume, your sessions with a psychiatrist?

Please put a tick in one of the following boxes:

a) Being wholly and utterly dependent on me, you were

a more convenient, less expensive option than a shrink   ☑

b) It was cathartic to take out my own demons on you   ☑

c) I set no value whatsoever on self-analysis   ☑

d) I was too cowardly to face my own monster of a mother   ☑

NOTE TO CANDIDATES

NB - When you have finished your paper please ensure that you have signed your name confirming yourself as author of your actions and turn it face down for the invigilator to collect.

RISING ABOVE

The other day - after more than half a century of what a doctor once called your 'uncertain behaviour' (an understatement surely so dry it all but constitutes a lie) - I had the strangest glimpse of how you must've been at sixteen or so: full of vivacity, humour and gaiety – all the qualities your mother leeched from you systematically all those years ago.

We were just saying goodbye as usual, at the back door by your small conservatory, in late summer, when I sensed that something else was happening too.

You made some joke or other, we laughed, and fleetingly, the two young women we had once been in different eras - met. The divide of time and our lamentable history mysteriously dissolved – leaving our younger spirits suddenly unencumbered and - in some way - free.

Was it that - in that moment - we suddenly felt how attuned, even how much alike, we might have been? And so, as our laughter faded, something unexpressed but part of that unalloyed delight spiralled like incense smoke ever upwards, caught in the early evening light.

TEA ROOM

Take Mum out to tea, she's seventy-seven, I'm fifty-four. Open fires, over-priced organic cake and bread. Brown smoke-stained paint, fringed lampshades hanging low and dark décor make up a gloomy interior which I usually hate but here find cosy and even rather quaint.

The tea arrives: a waitress stakes out the white crockery like a board-game, positions a sandwich and a slice of cake or two. We take up maroon napkins, the fire's flames hiss beside us in the grate; we chat at ease about this and that, your activities, my work, the family. I pour the tea; we stir it silently. "You know I've written a book about you, Ma?" I suddenly say. "Yes, I know." "How would you feel if I went ahead and published it?" "Of course you must, it's the least that I can do." She paused, "I doubt my friends would see it, they're mostly all dead."

There was a silence in which she caught my eye. "Was I really that awful?" I took her hand across the table: "You were, but it's all so long ago now and, as you know, I'm 54, life's gone on, it would be a little sad if I hadn't been able to let it go."

A pause. Her spoon adjusted gently on a saucer, one hand added to the other over mine, "I'm so sorry." The words hung in the air.

"You were bipolar, Ma, that's the thing. But the trouble was, you were also my mother, and I wasn't able, as a child, to separate the two." "I can see that." she replied. We smiled at one another, talked some more and then veered off to other things, finished our tea, and left.

Why did those few simple words, that fleeting two-second long apology mean so much so many decades late? I cannot calculate its value. It is without price, it is there, it has been said.

PRIMROSES

Remembering her moments of reprieve from mania or melancholy,
I recall how mother would eulogize the primroses each spring.
Was this just a mannerly response inherited from aged relations,
The brittle, string-pearl-adorned, tweed-skirted crew?
Or did these simple flowers genuinely entrance her,
An echo of what was, once, her absolute innocence?

I only know that now, each spring, the primrose moves me most,
Do I love them because of the way she did,
Her rapture in them the opposite of violence?
Occasionally, she'd pick a few frail stems to bring inside;
Selecting each one carefully, a rare stillness
In her concentration, beauty even - all disquiet laid aside.

EIGHTY

Somehow it has happened quickly, (my own life shooting by like images seen fleetingly from a train). Reduced in form, faint in voice, your hands tremble, and with unsure steps you shuffle forth. Everything has changed. Numbers and sequences have all gone blank, you insist that pin-numbers are a myth and money must be handed to you 1940s-style, when requested, at the bank.

Blunted by a small stroke, your confidence, your edge, and memory are now child-like, almost, at times, serene, your mental illness muted, perhaps in its own way, faded, its tragic origins eternally transmuted. This is, in some as yet ill-defined way for me, utterly extraordinary.

And other things astound in gentle & unfamiliar ways I find profound: you might take my face in your old hands, and in those eyes, and in that voice, I see and hear real joy, affection, even praise. And I can feel, across half a century of all that overt hostility, how much we lost, of trust, and generosity and love.

Now, in your last years, we share frequent teas, gossip and laugh, and you totter about, holding too-heavy tea-pots and refusing help. You are, generally, delighted by us all, disposed to joy even though things are moving out of reach: books are difficult to follow now, you sleep out ever longer tracts of time in front of the TV, (having researched, as ever, each programme zealously). You have become even more entranced by the Queen, whom you resemble, though she has never taken Lithium and so, though nine years your senior, is much stronger, a regal role-model for living longer. A new stair-lift stands unused in the hall, ("I'll use it for emergencies" you say) and a neighbour has your key. In the Memory Clinic you can only find, in the allotted minute, six words starting with the letter 'B'.

Stoic as more serious signs of your last stage assail you (arrhythmia and angina turn up frequently) you bravely mention that word 'death.' "Just in case" you say, "I'll take you to the peaceful place I'd like my funeral to be." ("Next time that heart thing happens, Ma," we said, "call **999**....")

It's ending after - roughly - eighty years - a life that both engendered and, for some time, persecuted mine. I'd like to've done the mother/daughter things that other people tend to do, but then I would not be me, and you would not, it follows, then, be you.

You said you felt massive relief when your own mother died, and she was not bipolar and only fifty-seven, (my age now). After you go, the contents of your house will be a mystery apart from all the obvious things that one can see. We were never so familiar or at ease that I could rifle through your stuff just as I pleased and I know that I'll feel furtive and plain wrong, more like a thief, going through your house, room by room, when you are, definitively, gone.

IN THE EMPTY HOUSE

Unchallenged, I'll trespass through your empty, furnished rooms.
I'll note each tidy polished thing awaiting probate,
The sale and dispersal to auction room, junk shop and bin.
But can your death be quantified? Measured, weighed?
Will your last words be spoken into the night,

And will I hear them?
Hold your hand, perhaps?
At your funeral, remain silent on the subject of your lasting legacy,
Just read kind thoughts in an unfamiliar hall
For those intimate strangers who thought they knew you well.

ALBUM

The odd loose photograph lies in the empty pages, at the back. I pull a sheet of polyfotos out and find us, at five, awaiting enlargement.

Sixty pairs of the same neat children gaze out from the black and white squares. Years ago you chose the better shots to send to relatives we hardly saw. We've been dressed for the occasion: I'm in a dark, smocked tartan dress, brother in a fair-isle, patterned jumper, three buttons done up at the shoulder. Our hair brushed into unfashionable partings, we're propped up on a narrow ledge, expressions unsure... (some pictures pick out mother's hand, child clinging on).

Bemused by so many shots of twins un-identical, I turn back to the album and us as thick-wristed babies adored in gardens by aunts in '50s dresses. Father putting his feet up, legs sticking out of the window of the Morris Traveller. Older now, taking uneasy hold of a sparkler; in duffle coats, sister crying in a garden snow-drift, Christmas parties. Colour shots begin, though faded now into the hue of that particular decade. Putting at Grandma's with a sawn-off golf club. Stung by wind-blown sand at the seaside. Trafalgar Square, a pigeon landing on our sister's head. There we are: snapped somewhere unfamiliar, feeding an animal.

I remember playing in those autumn leaves with other kids we didn't really know, joining in because that's what we were told to do. Prompted by vague feelings of content, someone fumbled for the camera. Forever out of focus, we had to hold the pose too long, I do not recognise the one you took of me, that day. Posterity and parents ask us to concoct a tidy joie-de-vivre: everyone looking over, into the future, grinning against their moods for the sake of those who turn the pages of the album now: rapt faces glow in celluloid's artificial sun, years summoned in a hint of cow gum with which, back then, you used to press each new print down.

Childhood's real verdicts end up somewhere else, but we must prove we tried: this is how 'all right' it really was: we gathered here, ate that, played this, followed some vague rules. But what dominates the past is how we felt, and who can chart a child's internal map? Still, here's another picnic in long grass, us: squinting at the lens, a paper plate upon each lap.

Of course, the sterile polyfoto pose remains the most unreal: mass-produced, date-stamped, trite little boxes of well-being, selected moments of official happiness to fire across the bows of unbelievers

and convince the relatives rank-and-file
that nothing can be untoward when, here,
the girl is seated in smocked tartan,
and the boy, fair-isle.

EPILOGUE

What fraction of a story told?
But let the matter rest!
From the haunted bower,
Strange flowers enough
Lie in these pages, pressed.

Burnt Dress

Joanna Murphy

Burnt Dress

© 2018 by Joanna Murphy

Published by The Heretic's Press
London
ISBN 978-0-9567920-8-2
Kindle ISBN 978-0-9567920-9-9

The Heretic's Press
www.hereticspress.co.uk